GUTFEELING

Instinct and
Spirituality@Work

**J. White
& Associates Inc.**

21 St.Clair Avenue East, Suite 400
Toronto, Ontario M4T 1L9
Tel: (416) 323-9282 Fax: (416) 323-9055

December 5, 2001

Mr. Peter Urs Bender
C/O TAG Publishing
108 – 150 Palmdale Drive
Toronto, Ontario   M1T 3M7

Dear Peter:

I have a "Gutfeeling" that this book will be a great success as it deals with the critical point of differentiation between Managers and Leaders.

Leaders and entrepreneurs use intuition as much as anything in divining vision, strategy and dealing with change. The quantitative bean counters be damned. That is how we ended up with Irrational Experience. Gutfeeling should be forced reading for every MBA student, but make their professors read it first.

As General Norman Schwartzkopf said often after the gulf War … "We always intuitively know the right thing to do. The hardest thing is to do it!"

Kind regards

Jerry White

McDonald's RESTAURANTS OF CANADA LIMITED
McDONALD'S PLACE
TORONTO, ONTARIO, CANADA M3C 3L4
(416) 446-3357 • FAX: (416) 446-3600

GEORGE A. COHON
FOUNDER
SENIOR CHAIRMAN

January 2002

Mr. Peter Urs Bender
TAG Publishing
108- 150 Palmdale Drive
Toronto, Ontario M1T 3M7

Dear Peter:

I thoroughly enjoyed reading your book Gutfeeling.

I remember well when I was a young lawyer in Chicago and I had a client that was interested in acquiring a McDonald's franchise for Hawaii. For the better part of a year, I negotiated with McDonald's on his behalf. I met with Ray Kroc, McDonald's Founder, frequently and I was pretty sure we had things in the bag. I had developed a good relationship with Ray; we understood each other, we trusted one another and we liked one another. I didn't see how he could possibly turn us down, but he did. Ray had his own way of doing things. He put great store in his instincts - instincts that had, by the way, served him very well. Ray's instincts were at work when he was on a flight one day and found himself sitting beside a bright energetic Hawaiian resident, who seemed to have everything Ray was looking for in a franchisee. They hit it off, and before the plane touched down, the Hawaiian franchise was gone.

Ray called me and said, "sorry about Hawaii, but the rights to most of Eastern Canada are open". My client, who had his heart set on Hawaii, was stunned and after talking with his wife, decided they would pass on Ray's offer of the rights to Eastern Canada.

When I called Ray to let him know of my client's decision, Ray said, "George, you don't want to be a lawyer for the rest of your life. Why don't you get involved". After talking it over with my wife, and listening to my instincts, I took him up on his offer....and, as they say, the rest is history. Thirty-four years later, we have over 1200 restaurants across Canada.

I'm glad that I listened to my Gutfeeling. If your book only helps a few to wake up that unknown power, it was worth writing.

Peter, I wish you all the very best.

Sincerely,

George A. Cohon

GAC/ns

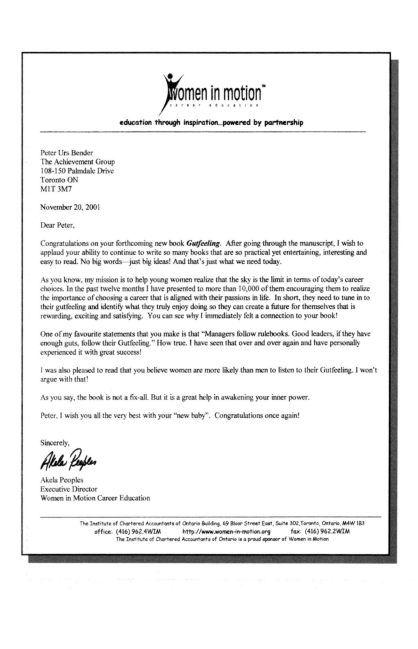

women in motion™
career education

education through inspiration...powered by partnership

Peter Urs Bender
The Achievement Group
108-150 Palmdale Drive
Toronto ON
M1T 3M7

November 20, 2001

Dear Peter,

Congratulations on your forthcoming new book *Gutfeeling*. After going through the manuscript, I wish to applaud your ability to continue to write so many books that are so practical yet entertaining, interesting and easy to read. No big words—just big ideas! And that's just what we need today.

As you know, my mission is to help young women realize that the sky is the limit in terms of today's career choices. In the past twelve months I have presented to more than 10,000 of them encouraging them to realize the importance of choosing a career that is aligned with their passions in life. In short, they need to tune in to their gutfeeling and identify what they truly enjoy doing so they can create a future for themselves that is rewarding, exciting and satisfying. You can see why I immediately felt a connection to your book!

One of my favourite statements that you make is that "Managers follow rulebooks. Good leaders, if they have enough guts, follow their Gutfeeling." How true. I have seen that over and over again and have personally experienced it with great success!

I was also pleased to read that you believe women are more likely than men to listen to their Gutfeeling. I won't argue with that!

As you say, the book is not a fix-all. But it is a great help in awakening your inner power.

Peter, I wish you all the very best with your "new baby". Congratulations once again!

Sincerely,

Akela Peoples

Akela Peoples
Executive Director
Women in Motion Career Education

The Institute of Chartered Accountants of Ontario Building, 69 Bloor Street East, Suite 302,Toronto, Ontario, M4W 1B3
office: (416) 962.4WIM   http://www.women-in-motion.org   fax: (416) 962.2WIM
The Institute of Chartered Accountants of Ontario is a proud sponsor of Women in Motion

W.K. BUCKLEY LIMITED/LTÉE

5230 ORBITOR DRIVE, MISSISSAUGA, CANADA L4W 5G7   TELEPHONE (905) 602-4422   FAX (905) 602-7561

January 14, 2002

Peter Urs Bender
108-150 Palmdale Drive
Toronto ON
M1T 3M7

Dear Peter,

The first time you told me about your new book *'Gutfeeling'*, I nearly fell off my bike! Maybe I'm working too hard at the Fitness Institute, I thought.

But after thinking about it, I have to agree with you. All good business decisions have to be based on logic and reason. But there is another factor. **Intuition** ---- what you call 'gut feeling'.

At W.K. Buckley Limited we're no different. Our Management Committee looks at new opportunities, analyzes them, and reflects on them. Then we vote. Reflecting on the analyses is one of the most important part of the process. It gives us time to have sober second thoughts, and to listen to our inner feelings.

Browsing through your new book, I must say you have some good simple advice on how to increase one's ability to listen to one's 'gut feelings'.

Peter, I wish you all the best with your new book and look forward to biking with you soon again!

Sincerely,

Frank C. Buckley
Chairman, W.K. Buckley limited

UNITED STATES · AUSTRALIA · NEW ZEALAND · CARIBBEAN · PAKISTAN · HOLLAND

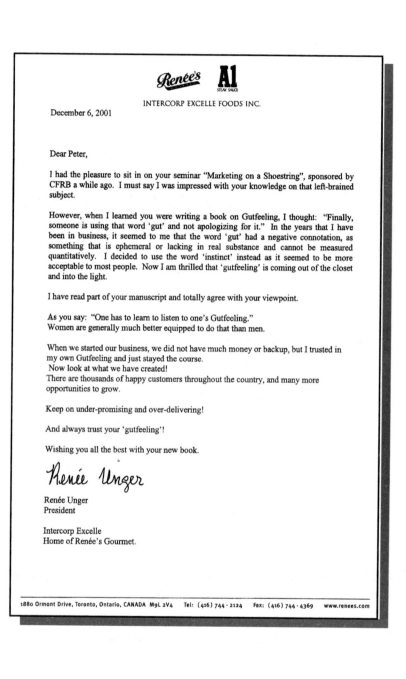

Renée's **A1**
STEAK SAUCE

INTERCORP EXCELLE FOODS INC.

December 6, 2001

Dear Peter,

I had the pleasure to sit in on your seminar "Marketing on a Shoestring", sponsored by CFRB a while ago. I must say I was impressed with your knowledge on that left-brained subject.

However, when I learned you were writing a book on Gutfeeling, I thought: "Finally, someone is using that word 'gut' and not apologizing for it." In the years that I have been in business, it seemed to me that the word 'gut' had a negative connotation, as something that is ephemeral or lacking in real substance and cannot be measured quantitatively. I decided to use the word 'instinct' instead as it seemed to be more acceptable to most people. Now I am thrilled that 'gutfeeling' is coming out of the closet and into the light.

I have read part of your manuscript and totally agree with your viewpoint.

As you say: "One has to learn to listen to one's Gutfeeling."
Women are generally much better equipped to do that than men.

When we started our business, we did not have much money or backup, but I trusted in my own Gutfeeling and just stayed the course.
Now look at what we have created!
There are thousands of happy customers throughout the country, and many more opportunities to grow.

Keep on under-promising and over-delivering!

And always trust your 'gutfeeling'!

Wishing you all the best with your new book.

Renée Unger

Renée Unger
President

Intercorp Excelle
Home of Renée's Gourmet.

1880 Ormont Drive, Toronto, Ontario, CANADA M9L 2V4   Tel: (416) 744 - 2124   Fax: (416) 744 - 4369   www.renees.com

GUTFEELING

Instinct and
Spirituality@Work

Peter Urs Bender
with George Hancocks

Edited by
John Robert Colombo

The Achievement Group

Published in 2002 by The Achievement Group
108-150 Palmdale Drive, Toronto, Canada M1T 3M7
416-491-6690

Stewart House Distribution Services Inc.
195 Allstate Parkway
Markham ON L3R 4T8
1-888-474-3478

10 9 8 7 6 5 4 3 2 1

CANADIAN CATALOGUING IN PUBLICATION DATA

Bender, Peter Urs, 1944-
Gutfeeling: instinct and spirituality @ work

ISBN 0-9695066-3-5

1. Success in business. 2. Self-actualization (Psychology)
I. Hancocks, George II. Colombo, John Robert
III. Achievement Group (Toronto, ON) IV. Title. V. Title: Gutfeeling.

BF315.5.B45 2002   650.1   C2002-900939-1

For
George Hancocks
A big man
with a big heart

Cover design: Mike Smith, Paulsen Communications
Text design: TAG

Visit Mr. Bender's website: www.Bender.ca
Printed and bound in Canada by Webcom.

A note to readers

The contents of *Gutfeeling* are presented in alphabetical style to make it easier for you to read and to access the thoughts contained in this book. Attention spans have diminished over the last few years. Readers don't want to waste their valuable time studying long, dull passages to pick up a few nuggets along the way.

The alphabetical format allows you to access the parts of *Gutfeeling* most interesting to you in the fastest possible manner. I have found that "dipping" helps you get into the spirit of a book quickly and without pain. There is no need to start at the beginning and read through to the end. This book has no beginning and no end. The beginning is where you want it to be. The end is when you've had enough for the moment. After all, the book's only job is to help you find more of your own Gutfeeling.

Late in life I discovered **the smarter I work, the luckier I get.** The smarter you read, the more you retain. Therefore, to get the most out of this book, as with any other, I highly recommend you read it with a pen or pencil in hand. Circle, underline, or even "x" out ideas you agree or do not agree with. As long as you don't go through the whole book and make an "x" on every page, it's okay with me.

I grew up with the idea that you do not write in a book. And I have to admit every time I start to read a book, I have to push myself to write in it. But there is no question that you will learn much more

Peter Urs Bender

when you underline and circle passages you think are of interest than if you only read them passively. When you then take the book out a few years later, you will be surprised to see what impressed you some time ago. Maybe you'll even wonder what impressed you so much that you felt you had to mark it!

George, my assistant, likes not only to underline and circle, but to use those new little colored sticky page markers to identify pages that intrigued him. He claims it provides his grandchildren with some insight into his thinking. He also says, "My grandchildren love to systematically remove them when they visit. It's a source of innocent merriment."

Remember that when you die, your family won't donate your books to the local public library. Nor will they hold an open auction. They'll have a garage sale! Then all your treasured books will go for $1.50 each (if you're lucky) to the nosy neighbors. That's life! Bon voyage and good luck!

Thank You

The one who has to be thanked first and foremost is George Hancocks. George has been my personal assistant for a long time now. He is one of those dedicated individuals who works long hours and puts into the job more than what's called for. He answers all my incoming calls on an ongoing basis. Over the years he has developed an outstanding relationship with all my clients and prospects. He looks after all my travels, schleps my books to the post office, my money to the bank, and even fixes my computer on weekends. In simple words, George is a man who always works hard. He under-promises and over-delivers. I learned a lot about life's philosophy from George. For instance, there are certain things which bother me, but I cannot change them. Therefore, why should I worry about them?

So why the book? That's a good question. The truth is that I thought George was under-utilized. He is a very skilled writer, having honed his talents and abilities over nearly five decades in the craft. As a matter of fact, he used to be an editor. So during the time the phone was not ringing, George and I talked about gut-feeling, intuition, spirituality, and instinct, and discovered we had a lot of common thoughts and feelings. When I told George how I felt about things in general and in particular, he simply turned on the computer and started writing down my thoughts. Then he looked at me and said, "Bender—you have another book!"

I would also like to say thank you to John Robert Colombo and his wife Ruth. They are the final editors of this work. Without their valuable input, *Gutfeeling* would not be what it is today!

Thanks are due also to Mike Smith, graphic designer, Paulsen Communications, for his fine work on the design of the cover and the front and end pages. Thanks also to Carole Elliott, director of communications for the Kidney Foundation of Central Ontario, Harold Morrison, writer, for reading the early manuscript and making helpful comments, and to Dr. Dwight Nelson of Regina for sharing many insights into his spiritual world.

A word of thanks is due, too, to Dr. Michael E. Rock, Emotion Quotient coach and facilitator. He gave us some excellent suggestions and deep insights into the thinking of Carl Jung. Thanks also go to Frank Baer, webmaster of *BeMoreCreative.com*. Finding his website was like finding the motherlode to every good quotation in history. There are many quotation sites on the web, but none as consistently useful or complete as Baer's. If you have a quote you think should be preserved, no matter from what humble source, send it to him. We'll all be eternally grateful.

But it is to you, my readers, I have to be most thankful. Writing is easy. Selling is tough! Thanks to you, most of my books are now bought as the result of referrals. One reader tells the other reader, and so it goes. Thanks for doing so.

My Gutfeeling also tells me to give credit to Frances, my wife of more than a quarter of a century—and still tells me not to put wet towels on the bed! To George Torok, my first licensee and co-author of *Secrets of Power Marketing*. To Dr. Robert Tracz, my co-author of *Secrets of Face-to-Face Communication*. To Eric Hellman, the man who transformed my seminar "Leadership from Within" into a first-class management book. And last, but not least, to Michael McClintock, the one who helped me the most with my first book, *Secrets of Power Presentations*, which is still the strongest of them all!

Gutfeeling

How to get the most out of this book

The reason I call this book *Gutfeeling* is because I have trouble with the word spirituality. Whenever I hear the word "spirit," it makes me want to pack up and go. I would have left at an earlier stage of my life. The minute anyone started to talk about "spirituality," or "spiritual values," I would simply turn away saying, "That's not for me."

That reaction seems strange to me now, but it's understandable. The minute one talks spirituality most think they're talking "religion." There are so many conflicting religions and religious beliefs floating around. The idea of becoming involved with their bureaucracies seems like a giant waste of time.

However, you can be spiritual, and not religious. The point I'd like to make is this: **Spirituality does not come from religion. Religion comes from spirituality**. A major definition of religion says it is "an institutionalized system of religious attitudes, beliefs, and practices." The emphasis is on the "institutionalizing process." You can be "religious" and be "spiritual" at the same time.

In fact, I believe it was religious practice that presented the aspect of spirituality in a way that made me turn away from it. Institutionalized spirituality tends to create a whole hierarchy of "beings" in order to explain its beliefs. Spirituality, one aspect of that, was presented as, "What happens when you die? Where does your spirit go?" Frankly, I believe when you die, you die. The show is over. End of story. However, assuming there might be a reincarnation—I will come back, no argument!

If you're a believer and involved in an organized religion, and find happiness through that, I think that's great for you. I might even envy you. My book can still help you to get more in touch with your Gutfeeling. What I'm outlining here has nothing to do with religion. It has to do with increasing your knowledge of yourself and of your inner feelings.

I don't worry about a final Judgement Day either. I am judged while I live. By myself and those around me. After I'm gone, no one is going to care. However, I do believe it's important to live a decent and ethical life. I am frequently (but not always) my own harshest critic, and I know others look at me and wonder how "good" I am. I like to believe others think well of me, and I certainly try to ensure they will. I try to live my life more like Mother Teresa than Al Capone, but after all, I am a man!

To the question of where your spirit goes when you die, I reply that I didn't feel completely free until, at some point in my life, I had the sense to quit asking questions for which there were no answers. Once you quit asking unanswerable (some would say meaningless) questions, you free yourself from a whole host of preconceptions about the nature of spirituality.

Let's take a concrete example. I use the computer every day in my work. At the end of the day I back up everything I've done that day on a zip disk. It's like magic when I take all those thousands of files I work with and use and watch them being transferred from one disk to another. Identical in every way to the original. Do I know how it's done? No. Do I need to know? Not really. I just use the technology that's available to me and say a silent thanks for its efficiency. Do I even need to ask how it happens? It would take me the rest of my life to understand the answer.

Like you, I use the telephone every day, too. When I dial the numbers across the city or around the world, it only takes seconds to ring. I know that if I've dialed correctly, the person I want (or at least his voice mail) will be on the other end of the line when the connection is made. Do I know how the phone system works? No. Do I care? No. I'm just content to use it.

When I travel I use the airplane. I know all about Bernouli's Laws of Aerodynamics, yet for the life of me, when that mammoth mass of metal heaves itself off the ground with me in it, I simply do not understand how it happens. Yet it does, and again, I am grateful. I don't question how it happens, and even though there are answers to many aspects of it, I am content to just "let it happen."

So what do I think spirituality is? It comes from deep within the human being. It's a universal feeling, and even if you've never had religious training, you still feel it. Everyone has it and feels it. What's more, it can be either positive or negative. (But I'm getting ahead of myself.)

There are three aspects of spirituality.

1. Energy
2. Gutfeeling (intuition, instinct, the subconscious)
3. Creativity

I'll explain what I mean by all three of these aspects of spirituality. But it's easier to tell you first what spirituality isn't.

It's not the spirituality of the relaxation gurus, or the spirituality of meditation. I'm a great believer that to live you need to relax. But relaxing can come in many different forms. You don't need to sit on a beach, watch the waves, and feel the wind on your body. Or lie in a field under the stars. You can do it within the confines of a hectic system. On a stressful busy day, you can do some deep breathing. You can do it in your car rushing to an appointment. In the elevator going to the big meeting, you can relax. Or on the way walking from a demanding boardroom session to lunch.

In fact, the Zen masters insist that the only way to relax is to do the job you're doing. For instance, if you're driving the car, do driving. (Think about all those individuals who try to "do" driving, "do" talking on the cell phone, and "do" drinking coffee at the same time.) Are you focused? No. You're distracted.

The very act of focusing intently, doing jogging for instance, enables you both to forget about your surroundings and to become more aware of them. You are focusing on the task you are doing, whatever that task is. That focus also includes everything around you that you need to assimilate to do the task well.

I often think we look at relaxing as something totally different from what we do every day. By doing so, we lose the relaxation that comes from focusing on the task at hand. Most think that to "relax" you must practice yoga or work at a hobby. Or do something very different from what you normally do. But you can only do yoga or a hobby for a fraction of your day or week. What do you do the rest of the time?

You have to sleep to live. The rain has to fall on the fields to make them green. You have to relax to get stronger. Relaxation is a break for the brain. But if you focus on one thing at a time you can work *and* relax at the same time. You can relax into your work. By doing so you become stronger.

So let's talk about the first aspect of spirituality called energy. You can't really put a finger on it, because energy *is*. Think of a car battery. When you're driving, the energy in that battery is kept topped up. There's enough to run all your car systems, with some left over for emergencies. When your car is parked, the energy is banked. But if you park too long, the energy diminishes and eventually the battery becomes depleted. It's not an exact analogy, but for our purposes it will serve.

Being human means we never stop running. We can slow down or speed up, but never "park," because if we do, quite simply, we die. The closest we come to "parking" is to sleep, but unlike the car battery, when we're idle in sleep we *generate* energy. Our inner battery is always on "charge."

I'm an eight-hour sleeper. Others are six- to- nine-hour sleepers. Some only need four hours a night. It doesn't matter how long we sleep. As long as the energy we generate is sufficient to make us productive human beings. The body needs, no question about it, a certain amount of sleep. The early bird gets the biggest worms,

Books by
Peter Urs Bender

National Best Seller

SECRETS OF
P·O·W·E·R
PRESENTATIONS

Peter Urs Bender

How to outpresent
**anybody,
anytime,
anywhere!**

National Best Seller

LEADERSHIP
FROM WITHIN

Peter Urs Bender

Stop blaming –
start leading yourself.

National Best Seller

SECRETS OF
P·O·W·E·R
MARKETING

**Peter Urs Bender
& George Torok**

You cannot–not market.
You market well or
you market poorly.

National Best Seller

SECRETS OF
FACE-to-FACE
COMMUNICATION

**Peter Urs Bender
Dr. Robert A. Tracz**

Take control of your
communication before
it takes control of you...

GUTFEELING
Instinct and
Spirituality@Work

Peter Urs Bender

Listen – you will hear it.
Watch – you will feel it.
Believe – you will
experience it.

Keynotes and Seminars
Peter Urs Bender

Leadership from Within
Leadership begins with leading ourselves.
Only then can we empower others.
Bender shows how to implement this
throughout a company to create
outstanding results.

Power Presentations
You are judged by appearances whenever
you present. How you communicate is
critical. Bender has helped thousands to
become outstanding presenters.

Power Marketing
You market poorly or well. You cannot
not market. This keynote/seminar is for
non-marketing professionals and
entrepreneurs.

Face-to-Face Communication
In this age of sophisticated communication technology, "old-fashioned"
one-on-one communication is often
neglected. Bender explains in an
entertaining way how we send signals
with our body.

Gutfeeling
Is it good looks, positioning, the right
name or education that produces
outstanding business people? They all
help. But Bender believes there is one
additional factor. The ability to listen
to your Gutfeeling.

For more information on keynotes
or in-house seminars please contact:

PAULSEN COMMUNICATIONS 1-800-479-2384

www.PeterUrsBender.com
416.491.6690

but the second mouse eats the cheese.

Sleep isn't the only way to generate energy. There are other elements that help you to recharge your energy. For instance, good feelings and a clear, positive vision. Even the weather can have an influence on your energy level. And if you have managed to come to terms with your "reason for living" (Why are we here? Why do we do things the way we do?) you will find that to be a great energy generator.

Many think there's a "ceiling" to the energy we generate and use. Imagine a frog in a jar covered with a glass top. He jumps and jumps but can't get past the lid. If he bumps his head once or twice, it prevents him from going higher. He quits trying, even if you remove the lid.

But we have more energy than we think. We see that in emergency situations. Suddenly we are doing things we never thought we could do. Or think of parents having young children. When you're older you experience and imagine yourself having less energy. But if you have a mission—something you absolutely have to do—your energy increases for doing it.

That's why I say that the whole idea of using our energy to the fullest involves "depleting" or using as much of it as we can. The more energy we use, the more becomes available to us. The more we spend, the more we create.

That's not an exaggeration. For example, if one is fatigued and yet does some exercises, the energy level rises. Just physically moving around the room or office, or doing anything at all physical—that little bit of exercise creates energy. If you jump a bit, for instance, you burn energy, but you also create it—so, in fact, energy will be created by energy.

You can use energy in a positive or in a negative way.

Negative energy depletes you faster. There is an old Chinese saying: **If you dig a grave for revenge, be sure you dig two.** Revenge involves real negative energy and it's no exaggeration to say if you're indulging in it, you're digging your own grave.

When we get upset about something, or worry about something, that activity burns negative energy. It's easy to say, "Don't worry about it," but as soon as you're in a cycle of worry—and everyone gets into one from time to time—you worry about it. When you worry, you burn negative energy. If you're in a negative job, relationship, or environment, you always want to get out of it. When relationships at home are not good, the environment is poor, flowers fade, and we lose the spark. That spirituality is negative and drains energy. The trick is to not fall into the trap.

Spirituality is contagious—both the positive and the negative kind. If you're with a person who has positive spirituality, you can feel it. The secret is to feel it within yourself and to sense that the universe is unfolding as it should.

If you're with someone who has negative spirituality, that negativism can drain you. I used to advocate that when you connected with someone who could only display negative spirituality, you should try to get out of that orbit. Today, I recommend not merely that you walk away, but that you run in the opposite direction as fast as you can. Negative spirituality will drain you right to the core.

Connect spirituality to energy. I think we've all got a positive energy charger. I don't think it's possible to explain what this energy is or where this energy comes from. We know when we have it, we know when we don't have it, and we know how to replenish it. What more do we need to know about it? We don't need to know how the television works, the phone, the computer, or the aircraft we fly.

The second aspect of spirituality is intuitiveness or Gutfeeling. I think we all have within us a feeling of what is right or wrong for us, for a project, or for our lives. We can't say where that feeling is located—whether in the stomach, the left upper part of your body, or the lower right. I think it's our job as humans to find that out, and to do that we need to learn to listen for it.

If someone says, "I don't have any Gutfeelings. Gutfeelings don't exist!" then it's difficult to prove it. A person first has to believe in intuition, then one has to find where it lies. Play with it. Albert Einstein called it "*Fingerspitzengefühl*" (on the tips of your fingers). It's well known, for instance, that you can often solve your problems by "sleeping on them." I even know a guy who believes the itch in his big toe. Listen when you have a feeling that something really will or really will not work. The more you can do that, the more you will be able to develop the feeling of that "gut."

I always remember seeing an interview on television with the great evangelist Billy Graham. Asked how he prepared his sermons, he answered, "I never prepare. I pray to God and when I do God gives me the words."

Now I personally do not believe that God in his or her heaven feeds him his words. But I do believe that Dr. Graham believes this to be true, and I know it works. Billy Graham knows so much about the Bible, he can hit thousands right over the head with his knowledge and belief and never have to stop and think about which words come next. He also brings to those sermons his own feelings, emotions, and practical experience. That's what makes him such a powerful preacher.

I think very highly of Dr. Graham. If Billy Graham believes God gives him his words, I wouldn't want to debate it with him because I believe **"as men think so shall it be."** I think it is the spirit of himself talking it out, and that is what I see as spirituality. Spirituality is a feeling that gives one the power to use our energy. To do more, and to become more productive. Spirituality, like leadership, comes from within. Everyone has it. Some are just more able to access it than others. I think that is because they have "experienced" it more often than others.

Think of your own life. If you think something doesn't exist, then for you it doesn't. If you say you don't have a problem, then in your own eyes, you don't. *Others* might think you have one. The person having the problem first needs to recognize he has one, or there's no chance of ever fixing it.

I also think we can be guided into becoming more aware of our intuitiveness or Gutfeeling. But you have to look at the person and the kind of background he was raised in. If one grew up in a very analytical, left-brain society, one probably is not all that familiar with Gutfeeling. If one grew up in a more creative, right-brain environment, then there's no question one knows and uses intuition and Gutfeeling more often.

I believe analytical thinking and intuitiveness complement each other. Take, for instance, a surgeon. If he says to you, "I have a Gutfeeling there's something wrong with you and I want to operate to fix it," you won't be too impressed. You expect your surgeon to be an analytical genius. A Gutfeeling is a personal intuition.

But I also bet that if you found the top surgeon in a hospital and started to talk with him, sooner or later he'd start talking about "Gutfeeling." He might say something like this: "When I did that operation I had the feeling I should look at such-and-such an organ. This, too, needed to be fixed. I did, and it worked. Why? Nobody knows." That surgeon just listened to his or her Gutfeeling.

I once knew a brilliant accountant. She was a genius at buying defunct or near-defunct companies, ferreting out information about them, and using it to negotiate the most advantageous purchase price possible. It was analytical, dry-as-dust stuff she was doing, but she wasn't a dry-as-dust person. She was, in my opinion, quite an intuitive person.

One day I asked her how she could possibly cope with all the dry analytical stuff she was doing and not go nuts. She replied that she found it fascinating to "get behind the figures." What did she mean, I asked. She said the figures led her to be able to draw a picture of the company's psyche! In other words, the numbers allowed her to create a vision of that company as it was in reality, and not as how it was perceived by its management. If the numbers didn't fit with what the management was telling her, she recreated the company, found all its hidden weaknesses, and was able to negotiate from strength.

One thing she said has stayed with me forever. She said the numbers enabled her to draw a portrait of that company, of its society, of its place in the community, of its importance to the country, and ultimately of the purchase value. That is analytical ability working hand-in-hand with intuition!

Creativity is the third aspect of spirituality. In its basic form, it's the ability to see things that don't yet exist. Your creativity enables you to make them happen. We all have it, starting very young.

Look at children. Give a child a stick and watch him or her play with it. In a child's eyes, it can become a plane, a car, a fairy or wizard's wand, a gun, a fiddle—you name it. To a child, that stick can become anything. This, I think, is the beginning of creativity, and as children we had it in full measure.

Watch youngsters coloring with crayons. If you ask a child to draw something and give it back to you, the response is often, "See what I drew here." You can't see what the child sees, but he insists this is you. Or the Man-in-the-Moon. The child sees all this quite clearly. That's where creativity starts.

Creativity is another aspect of spirituality and it can generate more energy for us. Usually it helps us to see things as better than they are. Creativity, in fact, is one of the few forces that can change reality.

If you look at high achievers, you will see they often went through very hard times, but they never saw those times as "bad." They always looked at the end result of what they were doing. They used their energy to create a better environment for themselves. They persisted, and one day it all came together for them. Others, looking at this situation, called them "lucky."

Good ideas come when one is in harmony with oneself, and here I'm talking straight business. A new product, a new idea in marketing, or a new idea in selling or speaking comes when one is in harmony with oneself. This I call **Spirituality@Work**. It comes from somewhere within, but we can't put a finger on it.

This book will give you ideas on how to develop your spirituality. It may sound strange to talk about developing something that I say is inborn—but who do you know who can play the violin, ride a bike, or drive a car by the "think method"? Spirituality does not often fall on one full-blown from heaven. Most of us have it within us, but we have to work at it. How to get the most from it is the message and the method that I hope to leave you with.

So what I have done in this book is the following. I have used many familiar business words and looked for the Gutfeeling that is part of them. Your job is to wake up your own Gutfeeling and make full use of its power.

Aberglauben

Negative superstition reinforces bad luck!
—Peter Urs Bender

Aberglauben is the German word that means "superstition." Be careful what you wish for. Your wish might be granted!

I have also read that you become the thing you most think about. However, I must say that is not always true because during the early part of my life I thought mainly about women...

I don't believe in superstition. Except on Friday the 13th, which is my lucky day. And I'm careful what I wish for. Also, I never walk under ladders. Something might fall on me!

Actually, what I do believe is that you *should* be superstitious, if it brings you luck! Superstition, seen in that light, is your spirit talking to yourself. I like to think of it as your subconscious talking to your conscious, and telling you to "be careful." I also like to think of it as your unconscious talking to your conscious and telling you to "take a chance."

Thought of in that way, *Aberglauben* is a positive force. It's a great way of putting you in touch with your own spirit. We all get a little superstitious from time to time. Even if we don't *believe* in it with all our hearts.

Carl Jung, for instance, talked about synchronicity, which is really another way of saying "coincidence." What we think of as coincidences may *seem* to happen, but they occur when as Jung might say "the inner and the outer are the same." Whatever happens is whatever happens. That we recognize it when it coincides with our thoughts is a "gift," something not sought but found anyway.

I heard the story of a teenager named Pat who had a very old car. Like many pieces of old mechanical equipment, it was quirky. "Things" would happen to it at the oddest moments, almost always when it was least expected. On Friday the 13th, while racing to an appointment, all four tires (and the spare) blew out, one right after the other.

It wasn't superstition that blew the tires. Pat knew they were due for replacing and had done nothing about it. The "coincidence" could have happened on Monday the 1st. But it happened on Friday the 13th. It taught Pat a lesson. If we let things slip then blame it on superstition, we're kidding ourselves.

We build our problems step by step. If we have one problem, we're likely to have another. I think repetitive "happenings" are like self-fulfilling prophecies. If we let ourselves think that way, we may already have created the conditions so they will happen.

In my book *Leadership from Within*, I say, **"Your past was perfect to get you where you are today."** Your "character" didn't just happen. It was built, brick by brick—by you—as the result of your experiences, and your reaction to them. That's the reason we call the heartbreaking, upsetting, frustrating experiences that happen to us Character Building!

Things that happen to you have a reason for happening—and that reason lies within ourselves. As Shakespeare has Cassius say in *Julius*

Caesar. "The fault, dear Brutus, is not in our stars, but in our-selves...."

Superstition can be *good* for you if you react to it or manage it in a positive way. But you must be *aware* of what it is. Realize it's like a "still, small voice" suggesting a course of action. For instance, I always cross my fingers behind my back before making an important presentation. Then I make a good one. It works!

If you utilize superstition from that point of view, it's a power for good. But if you allow it to claim you, if you believe every superstition you've ever heard, you're headed for trouble.

*Are you allowing yourself to be moved
by superstition in a negative way?*

Aboriginal

The Soul is the voice of the body's interests.
— George Santayana, philosopher

Aboriginal cultures have many "spiritual guideposts." Smoke signals, bird figures, dream images, animal guides, animated drawings—all of these draw attention to the spiritual world. They also point the direction for human action. But because these guideposts are so very different from those found in non-native cultures, we often call aboriginal cultures "primitive." We belittle them and feel they're not as real as ours.

There's an old story that compares the Eastern custom of putting food on graves with the Western custom of placing flowers on gravesites. One observer asked his Eastern colleague when he thought his ancestor would eat the food left out for him. "The same time yours will smell the flowers," was the answer. The moral: Cultures use different symbols to acknowledge their beliefs in the world of spiritual values.

If you look objectively at aboriginal cultures, you see immediately they promote both individual and collective fulfillment. Their values don't endanger the planet, and group members are able to live together, mostly in harmony.

If you think culture is playing the piano, driving a Porsche, or dancing at the Ritz, your view of aboriginal cultures is probably that native peoples are losers. Yet real happiness can come from the ability to recognize Gutfeeling. Native cultures appear to be good at that. Perhaps they are not so primitive after all!

When you are in harmony with yourself,
how do you feel in your stomach?
What's your Gutfeeling?

Accounting

Logic is the key to an all-inclusive spiritual well being.
—Marlene Dietrich, movie star

Accounting is something we all are familiar with. Without it, one would be unable to run a business properly. It's possible to fumble along for a while with a notebook, a good memory, and a boxful of receipts—but a business won't go anywhere using those methods.

Real accounting, the type invented by the Italians a few hundred years ago, is a system. You have to work at it to make it work, and you have to follow its rules to make sense of its results. At its best, it's a predictor of business events; at its worst, it's a mental strait-jacket. (Of course, it's said that old accountants never die—they just lose their balance.)

Spirituality is similar. It's a system, too. It doesn't drop like manna from heaven. It starts as a feeling, a tingling, a gut instinct, an intuition. It requires you to listen to it. To be aware of it. To work at it until it begins to "bloom." At its best it's a modifier of behavior; at its worst it, too, is a straitjacket.

How do spirituality and accounting mesh? At first glance it seems they don't. Accountants are often analytical people. Reason and logic are their tools. They don't seem to rely on intuition much, and seldom acknowledge a belief in spirituality.

But…spirituality is also built on a structural base when you understand it. It requires logic and reason to operate. Do you think someone who knows nothing about accounting comprehends it instantly? Understanding and the ability to use accounting require training and experience. So does spirituality.

But both systems appear very illogical if you don't understand them. As a matter of fact, anything you don't understand in life is very complicated and often seems illogical. Computers, chess, card games, to name a few. But as soon as you gain some understanding, and begin to work at a system—it becomes easy. You might even begin to understand its logic!

Look again at accounting and spirituality—there is a system to accounting; there is a system to spirituality. In general, the accountant does not see the system of spirituality, and I think spirituality does not often see the system of accounting. But they do work together.

That's because of the system that is the basis of both of them. It helps those who are confused get less confused, and those who already have talent to excel. In my book *Secrets of Power Marketing*, I talk about the importance of a system. I say that if you have a talent for a task and a system to approach it, you can perform the task easily. If you don't have a talent and you have no system, don't try the task.

>The system for accounting is in numbers.
>The system for spirituality is in meditation.

If you cannot see the pattern, try to feel the pattern.
Feel for it. It's there.

Achievement

Do something so well that the world
will pay you money to see you doing it again.
— *Walt Disney, father of Mickey Mouse*

Levers require two pieces to function at all. The lever itself, and the fulcrum—the place you rest it to get the work performed. The fulcrum is necessary. A lever simply cannot work alone.

If you look at anyone who has performed outstandingly, you will find an unsung team that helped the individual reach that height. Behind every great woman, there is a great man! The achiever may not even realize how much he or she owes to the "team fulcrum," but the debt is there.

In business, leverage is known as the ratio of debt to equity. It's what you owe as opposed to what you own. If a business is "highly leveraged," that means it has a high ratio of debt to equity. Every high achiever has, whether recognized or not, a highly leveraged life.

Gutfeeling, harnessed properly, should be your lever to great accomplishments. It's you own personal equity. You can build it and use it. With help from a personal fulcrum you can do even more amazing things.

Be analytical. Scrutinize situations—from stock market purchases and real estate investments to critical personal decisions. Take personal advice from friends and family members you trust. But for the final decision, listen to your inner voice, to your Gutfeeling.

If you look back on your life, you will discover that many times you were forced to wait to make a decision. Then, suddenly, you either got cold feet or decided to go ahead. That was Gutfeeling at work.

The objective is to leverage your decision-making process by consciously listening and using your inner voice—with a little help from others.

Do you remember the first time you experienced that Gutfeeling as a child?

Annual Meeting

*It is far more important to be able to hit the target
than it is to haggle over who makes a weapon or who pulls a trigger.*
—Dwight D. Eisenhower, U.S. president and Army general

There's nothing more boring than the Annual General Meeting of a company that is holding one just because it has to. Even worse is attending the AGM of one that doesn't know where it's going. Annual meetings can be a real pain in the neck.

If you want real progress, whether on the corporate or on the personal level, you need to meet at much more frequent intervals. Hold employer/employee meetings every three months. Personally, examine yourself at least once a month.

The whole purpose of these meetings is to check if we're on target. For the best personal results, however, set aside a few minutes for yourself every day. Make sure you know where you want to go. Say hello to yourself every night and every morning.

Annual meetings are like New Year's Resolutions. They're fine, but if you want results, make every day January 1.

When did you last do a checkup from the neck up?
When did you last give yourself heck because you weren't on target?

Arbitrage

*Look at me: I worked my way up from nothing
to a state of extreme poverty.*

— Groucho Marx, comedian

The essence of arbitrage is buying and selling on two different markets, says Jerry White in his *Dictionary of Finance and Investment Terms*. "For example, an arbitrageur buys one contract of gold in the Zurich market and sells one contract of gold in the New York market at the same time. He locks in a profit because the price on the two markets is different. Even after currency conversion is taken into account. (The arbitrageur's selling price is higher than the buying price.)"

Gutfeeling is a little like buying in one market and selling in another. And listening to your Gutfeeling is not always easy.

For instance, your intuition might feel positive in one way, negative in another. You must learn to analyze where those feelings reside. Like the arbitrageur, you have to determine where the "profit" is and bet on the feeling that will lead you to correct action.

But let's be clear about it. Your Gutfeeling is not infallible. Nothing is 100% in life—except death, taxes, and rainy days. Your job is to make the most of a less-than-perfect situation.

You have to identify where your positive Gutfeeling resides. You may even have two different Gutfeelings. Your emotions may pull you one way, your physical sensations another, and your rational thoughts in a third direction.

It's important to decide where in your body your emotions, sensations, and thoughts reside. For instance, you may hear a thought quite clearly: "I'm not sure what to do about this."

Do you feel yourself physically hesitating or pausing? Does your stomach flutter? Your head ache?

Do you feel emotionally disturbed and unsure? Your instinct may be telling you, "This is not a good idea." Or it may say to you, "Go ahead. Everything will be okay."

These feelings will reside somewhere, that you can be sure of. Your job is to locate them, weigh them, and like the arbitrageur, make a decision that will profit you.

When did you last have different Gutfeelings?
For instance, different ones in your stomach,
your sense of smell, your feelings, and your intuitions?

Balance Sheet

*A balance sheet is a statement of condition
at a particular time.*

—Jerry White, business consultant

A balance sheet lists your assets and liabilities, and shows your net worth as of a given date.

If you want to increase your net worth, you have to increase your assets or reduce your liabilities. It's the same with spirituality, as with a balance sheet. You cannot just say, "Gimme more!"

The emphasis is on "doing." If you don't do these things, I guarantee you it will not come and you will not increase your spiritual net worth!

Your balance sheet as an employee lists these as assets: your skills, knowledge, enthusiasm, and the time you offer to your employer. You also carry liabilities: the cost to maintain you as an employee, your salary or hourly cost. It seems fairly simple to understand, then, that to increase your salary or hourly wage, you have to increase the assets you bring to your company. You do not get paid on what you're worth.

What assets do you bring to your spiritual balance sheet?

Belief

When will power and imagination have a conflict it's always imagination that wins.

—Maxwell Maltz, plastic surgeon

We all believe. We all have a belief system, whether we like it or not. Whether it's right or wrong. Beliefs can be as simple as when you're behind the wheel of your car and you see a green light, you can "GO." You believe that. You can still be killed. Some other guy might go through the red in the other direction. But you still believe in the "rules of the road."

If you're smart, you're careful, though. You look left and right. You don't have to be such a total "believer" that you can't express doubt or be a little more on the doubting than on the believing side.

We have many systems that we "believe" are okay and we do what the system tells us to. It's just built into us to perform that way.

The older I get, the more I believe in what Maxwell Maltz said in his classic book *Psycho-Cybernetics*:

"A human being always acts and feels and performs in accordance with what he imagines to be true about himself and his environment."

Spirituality is a deep belief in oneself. If you want to achieve something, you have to believe you can do it before you actually can. If a person says he has no belief system, that's a person who cannot achieve greatness.

Spirituality is the same. You have it and it will come out if you let it. If you can work with it, you have the possibility to achieve more.

When did you last challenge will power with imagination?

Black Monday

The difference between playing the stock market and the horses is that one of the horses must win.

—*Joey Adams, comedian*

Mondays, traditionally, are bad days. Many heart attacks occur Monday morning. It's a heavy day for traffic accidents, too. In our culture Monday becomes Doomsday. Compare that with Friday, when TGIF (Thank God It's Friday) becomes the mantra. Why?

That Monday is always "black and blue" is a wry commentary on the way we live. If you hate your job so much you dread going back to it at the beginning of the week, what are you doing about it?

There were two Black Mondays in the last two decades of the 20th century, one on 19 October 1987, and one almost exactly ten years later on 27 October 1997. They were days when investors felt like jumping out of the windows of tall buildings.

I know it's one thing to say, "I hate this place," and something else to say to yourself, "I'm going to get out of here." But if every Monday is a Black Monday, start taking steps to get out of the environment you're in. Actively look for other opportunities. Remember, if you do what you've always done, you'll get what you've always gotten!

One of the best jobs a friend of mine ever got resulted from not answering the ritual question "How are things going?" with the traditional "Okay." At the time he was so fed up he spontaneously replied, "Rotten!" When asked why, my friend poured it all out, and suddenly he was being offered alternative employment. His Gutfeeling took over. He told me he could feel it urging him to make a break with the past.

Don't waste your time doing something you don't like. Life is too short. Remember, you can leave any job in the world and someone will be glad to take it over. You are not irreplaceable. Don't worry. Your company won't fall apart.

Use Monday as your regeneration day. How? Believe in your job and look forward to doing it. Whether you run a business, clean floors, or drive a bus, listen to your Gutfeeling. Should you do your job or get out of it? Answering the question the right way could be your first step to happiness. Let your Gutfeeling tell you how.

Is Monday the beginning of a fresh new week,
or the sad ending of the weekend?
What are you going to do about it?

Business values

If business counts only on its profits it is a very poor business.
— Henry Ford, industrialist

Very few businessmen have mused openly about the connection between business and spirituality. Henry Ford was one who did. The same idea appears in M.P. Follett's 1924 book *Creative Experience:* "The divorce of our so-called spiritual life from our daily activities is a fatal dualism."

What Ford and Follett are both saying is that making a profit—the bottom line—is not the only aim of business, just one of them. True, it's important to make a buck, and the creation of profit through a business is very important. But business is a daily activity. The business person who applies all his or her talents—and this includes spirituality—to the business is both a better business person and a better individual.

In a sense, everything in life is a business—government, police, hospitals, doctors, teachers, and pop artists. When spirituality becomes a business, it becomes a religion. We don't live in a state of individual anarchy (although it sometimes feels like it). We couldn't have a society or a business of any kind if everyone went off in a different direction and there was no cooperation at all.

We know we are spiritual beings, even if we don't always understand that part of ourselves, or are out of touch with our spirituality. Spirituality, says Christina Baldwin, in her book *Life's Companion:
Journal Writing as a Spiritual Quest,* "is the sacred centre out of which
all life comes, including Mondays and Tuesdays and rainy Saturday
afternoons in all their mundane and glorious detail....The spiritual
journey is the soul's life commingling with ordinary life." So business and spirituality are inescapably intertwined, whether we like it
or not. We live. We have to work to live a full life. We're "taking care
of business" at the same time.

Are you working just for money, just for fulfillment, or for both?

Cats and dogs

Dogs come when they're called;
cats take a message and get back to you.

—*Mary Bly, feminist and author*

One thing I love about cats is their independence. One thing I hate about cats is their independence.

That contradictory nature is the essence of cats. How does it relate to Gutfeeling? I think it makes us aware that cats are sensitive to emotion, to feelings of any sort. They remind us that we should be, too.

From early Egyptian times, cats have been both adored and feared. They were among the first animals to be domesticated. Yet they have never truly been domesticated at all. They willingly accept all donations of food. But even on a full stomach, they don't hesitate to hunt. They have never lost their wild, instinctual nature. They are constant reminders to us that there is always "something beyond."

They have always been associated with spirituality. The Egyptians thought of them as guardians of the dead. Though dreaded as "familiars" of witches in the Middle Ages, cats have nevertheless retained their own identities.

The original meaning of "familiar" is "attendant," often to an honored person. Today we realize that witches were often sensitive, educated, intuitive people living in a cruel, ignorant, insensitive society. A "familiar" was defined, even then, as "an intimate" or a spirit embodied in an animal to attend, serve, or guard. What association could have been more natural or intuitive!

Have you ever watched cats with people who don't like them? Inevitably, they will gravitate to that person. Why? I think they sense hostility. Because they are among the most comforting of creatures, they cannot bear to sense dislike, and immediately try to overcome it. They always try to make the person who doesn't like them feel better.

Far-fetched? Maybe. But simply stroking a purring cat can result in a feeling of tranquility.

Dogs, too, have been associated with spirituality from ancient times. Their mummified bodies, like those of cats, were placed in Egyptian tombs to accompany their masters into eternity. Where cats are independent, dogs are affectionate. It is not by accident that they have acquired the label "man's best friend." To a dog the master is always Napoleon or Queen Victoria.

You can feel affection for cats, but rarely friendship. Cats are too aloof, too centered in themselves. With dogs, however, humans can form lifetime attachments. Indeed they have frequently been featured in literature for their skills and abilities as human companions. When a dog trusts you, he trusts you completely. Cats remain always distant.

Despite their different natures, cats and dogs can put us in touch with the "otherness" of our own natures. Both (and other pets for that matter) help us to get a grip on our Gutfeeling.

Have you tried relating to your Gutfeeling by relating to animals?

Chocolate

Most women love chocolate more than sex.
— Belgian proverb

Anything you like to do must give you satisfaction. It may be momentary or long term—but it must fulfill one of your needs. For instance, the taste of chocolate makes most women feel good for a short time.

If you don't like chocolate, you won't get any satisfaction from it. Therefore you probably wouldn't even touch it. You might like food, work, alcohol, nicotine, sex, or whatever. There are many interesting and exciting things to satisfy your needs. We're human.

Gutfeeling is similar to chocolate. If you listen to it, it can make you feel good. But if you don't get any satisfaction from it, you won't believe in it.

Nevertheless, we agree human beings strive for satisfaction. We also have to agree we all have feelings. Can we harness and make use of them?

When was the last time you consciously asked yourself,
"What gives me satisfaction?"

Chutzpah

Chutzpah is unmitigated gall, like the fellow
who murders his parents and then appeals
to the jury for mercy because he is now an orphan.
—*Leo Rosten, commentator*

You can have chutzpah without knowing how it's spelled! People who do outstanding things have chutzpah. Anyone who has achieved anything must have had some chutzpah—even if he or she doesn't know the word.

The dictionary seems divided over meanings, but favors "presumptuous audacity"…"disregard of constraints commonly imposed by convention or prudence" or even "shameless insolent disregard of propriety or courtesy." In essence, it means having the nerve, the will (and sometimes even the stupidity, as in "Fools step in where angels fear to tread") to take the risks others run from.

If you've never taken any risks, you likely haven't experienced chutzpah. Perhaps you never will. If you don't enjoy traveling, art, or music, you likely never will—until the day comes when you have the chutzpah to do so.

It takes presumptuous audacity for a secretary to tell the president his fly is open! It takes chutzpah for a whisky-drinking, tobacco-chewing cowboy to attend the opera or ballet.

For certain people it takes chutzpah just to listen to their Gutfeeling, either because it's a feeling they distrust and feel uncomfortable with, or simply because they don't believe in it.

Others listen to their Gutfeeling all the time.

If you've never listened to your Gutfeeling, you could use some chutzpah. Just take your courage in hand and do it, even if you feel silly. The results are worth it.

When was the last time you did something
your common sense told you was outrageous?
(Try it: You'll like it!)

Communication

To be twice as powerful — use half the words.

— Peter Urs Bender

To everything there is a structure. Everything has its rules, whether they come in instruction manuals or not.

Communication is one of those activities we cannot not do. If we are silent, say nothing to anyone, we communicate. What do we say? "Stay away from me. I don't want to/can't talk. I'm shy/secretive/alone." Maybe that's not true, but that's what we're communicating. Saying nothing is not an option.

On the other hand if we're too talkative, can't keep our mouths closed, we're communicating the opposite message. "Don't tell this person anything—unless you want the world to know it."

It is useful to ask the question, "Why is communication so important?"

I think there are three reasons why it is so important for human beings to communicate effectively.

First, we need to share information.
Second, we need to issue commands.
Third, we need to share common feelings.

The first two are pretty obvious. But the need to share feelings is as deep as Gutfeeling itself. My favorite example of it is a familiar one that occurs every day in driving down a busy street. I stop my car at an intersection. A pedestrian is planning to step in front of my vehicle. The pedestrian, a complete stranger, glances at me, catching my gaze. I look back and nod. The nod is the bare bones of a message, but the message is vital. It communicates the following information: "I see you. I know you will be stepping in front of my car. I will not run over you."

I keep recalling the words of the philosopher Marshall McLuhan who said, "The medium is the message." The medium—the telephone, an email message, a conversation in an office—is important. But the content of the message is just as important, and McLuhan saw you can't separate one from the other. It's the sharing of information, the issuing of orders, and conveying fellow feeling. In that respect communication is both as elusive yet as instinctive as Gutfeeling.

My first book, *Secrets of Power Presentations*, outlined a straightforward and practical system for making presentations and public speaking—in other words, for communicating publicly. Only later did I realize the importance of the connection between talent and system.

By the time I wrote my next book, with George Torok, it had become clear to me that talent and system are inseparable. I realized that a person with talent but no system could succeed. But a person with both talent and a system would gain maximum results on a repeatable basis. *Secrets of Power Marketing* showed that even a person with little talent but with a consistent system could gain regular and improving results.

Dr. Robert Tracz and I emphasized that systematizing any activity can help you to excel at it. We also laid out some of the basic steps for clearer, more powerful one-on-one communication in *Secrets of Face-to-Face Communication.*

Structures and systems and the talent to use them are very important. But to be really effective you need both structure *and* the ability to listen to your Gutfeeling. That's the only way you can truly begin to communicate openly.

If all you have is a system, you'll be like Picasso painting by numbers. As a matter of fact, it was Picasso who said, "Art without a system is a waste." Without Gutfeeling your communication won't have much life. Listen to your Gutfeeling and let go!

What was the best conversation you ever had?
Was it scripted word for word, or intuitive and spontaneous?

Computers

When computers were first invented, they could perform only four tasks: add, subtract, multiply, and divide. Even that seemed like a miracle. It was the beginning of our ability to compress time.

Today, it's hard to believe that the greatest revolution in human history began in a couple of garages. Bill Gates came from nowhere to make his unknown company Microsoft the dominant force in software and to become the wealthiest man on the planet.

Or how about that guy named Jobs? He made an Apple with a bite out of it the symbol for his company, and Macintosh the internationally recognized name of the machine. Is it symbolic that Eve, who offered Adam the original apple in the Garden of Eden, "partook of the Tree of Knowledge"? Does it mean that a woman is always the first to know what it's all about?

Then came the game stage. Humans competed against the machine in breathtaking and fantastic contests. Humans love to play! Even chess has become computerized. Checkers and card games are standard fare. There is an inherent logic to games, and we readily adapted the computer to challenge us.

It was only one step beyond that for computers to "learn" from their "mistakes" in competition. It seemed that computers had been given the ability to "think."

Yet what was really happening? Some of our most creative minds had learned how to create these scenarios. Their programs (really a slice of their thinking) offered the rest of us the opportunity to match ourselves against the best and brightest of our race. They helped us to learn quickly what other, smarter people already knew—as long as it could be logically structured.

But the great difference between our brain and the computer's circuit boards is that most of our decisions are based on emotion. I really question whether we will ever be able to create computers to use emotion as a factor in decision-making, all science-fiction scenarios aside.

Yes, there are similarities between the human brain and the computer. Both operate on the same GIGO principle. Garbage in, garbage out! Both are capable of logical thinking. But the computer is incapable of thinking in any other way.

If you look at the important personal decisions you make in your life you will find they are mostly based on emotion. They may be justified by logic. But they begin with feeling. The best decisions are based on Gutfeeling—your internal sense of the "rightness" of your action.

No computer "senses" its actions are "right" or "wrong." A computer acts as a computer acts. If you have ever tried to overcome the logic of a computer's circuits, you will understand it cannot be done. You can "trick" it into doing something you want it to do. But to do that you must create a logical path for it to go in the direction you want.

Humans can be "coaxed" that way, too. But more often the appeal to emotion will win the day. To claim to act only on logic, as machines must, is to ignore half the capabilities our brains possess.

A computer is like fire. It makes a wonderful servant but a terrible master! They are here to stay, to use. But the element of emotion in human thought cannot be replaced by logic.

Next time you make a decision,
ask yourself how much of it was based on logic
and how much on Gutfeeling.

Credits

If you don't know the value of money, go and borrow some.
— Benjamin Franklin, scientist and statesman

Since the 1960s, every adult has had a credit card. Today you also have a debit card. Before the Sixties credit and debit were there. You just couldn't access either as easily as we do today, nor could you manipulate either as quickly.

Since the Sixties you've probably discovered the more you spend the more credit you'll be granted, as long as you pay regularly.

Spirituality is like that, too. The more you experience it—the more you will gain. The more you are able to get that "Gutfeeling"—the more of it you will experience.

To increase your credit line, you have to increase your spending. To get more rewarding spiritual experiences, you have to learn to trust your Gutfeelings. You cannot touch them the way you would a tangible object. You have to give yourself the assurance and the belief that you can feel them.

If you ask anybody who does a lot of believing in Gutfeeling, you will see he or she started up somewhere. You do the same as with your credit card. Begin with a few hundred dollars, and increase your limit gradually.

Roger Bannister, the first human to run the four-minute mile, had to believe it was possible to do it. Almost all the experts didn't. But Bannister knew he was himself physically fit to do it. He measured his performance over a long period of time. Then he went for it— and succeeded. He set about it rationally, measuring himself against the current standard. Then he pushed himself just that little extra bit every time until he knew (not just felt) he was capable of doing it. After him, hundreds of runners succeeded in doing it.

When did you last exceed your limit
(when others said it couldn't be done)?

Debit

To get credit you must spend. To get debit you must have.

— Old Swiss saying

Debit and credit are two sides of the same coin. Debit is your own money. Credit is someone else's. My wife often calls me handsome. Hand some money! Your debits are my credits and my credits are your debits, not as in many things where what's yours is mine and what's mine's my own!

With debit you don't pay interest. You pay for your purchase up front, and you spend as you need. The money is in your bank account, however. It doesn't come from thin air. It comes because you worked for it. You built up a reserve on which you can call as you need it. It's not like credit, where you are spending money you don't have. A tax on your future.

Spirituality is like debit. You can "spend" your spirituality once you've got it, but you can't create it with a debit card, any more than you can create cash in the bank by wishing to. You work for it, and then you bank it or save it, and use it as necessary. But the only way you can create debit (or spirituality) is to work at it. The more you work, the more likely you'll be to achieve it.

Alexander Graham Bell said, "The most successful men in the end are those whose success is the result of steady accretion." He added, "It is the man who carefully advances step by step, with his mind becoming wider and wider—and progressively better able to grasp any theme or situation—persevering in what he knows to be practical, and concentrating his thought upon it, who is bound to succeed in the greatest degree."

Are you consciously increasing your spiritual reserves?

Dreams

Dreams, imagination, fantasies, and movies
can have the same impact as reality.
Just think of Hitchcock's **Psycho.**

— *Peter Urs Bender*

We all dream. The question is, do we remember our dreams? Dozens of books have been written on how to interpret and remember dreams.

I don't put too much store in the value of reading or explaining dreams. But I do believe that part of our daily thinking gets dumped into our subconscious. If there's too much negative stuff in that thinking, it can ultimately affect our actions.

Big events, positive or negative, can influence our sleep, and cause funny dreams. Those dreams must be trying to tell us something.

Assume you have a big decision to make. Take it to bed with you. Don't think about it all night. Just sleep on it. It could be that in the morning a solution is easier to arrive at. Just try it out.

Many people think they find the answer in their sleep. I think it's the relaxation that allows your brain time to review the material. And then, in the morning—in a split second—your brain solves the puzzle.

The longer you actively think about a problem, the worse it often gets. Think of the ancient puzzle of the Gordian knot. For centuries sages puzzled over how to unravel it. Alexander the Great's solution was simple. He just cut it.

Anybody can make something relatively simple into something very complex. Just keep on dwelling on it. It's called "worrying your problem to death." That's because one keeps adding complexities until one has virtually lost sight of the original problem.

Remember, analysis is good. As a matter of fact, it's very important. But you can overdo it. Take your problem to bed. Relax with it, rather than think about it.

One very important aspect of dreams, according to Swiss psychoanalyst Carl Jung, is that they compensate for the one-sidedness of the conscious mind.

For example, if you are a conscious extrovert, you will be introverted at the unconscious level, and vice versa. If at the conscious level you are analytical, at the subconscious level you will feel strongly.

To round out your personality, you must let the subconscious part of your psyche into your consciousness. This is precisely what happens in dreams.

Dreams are the channels through which the unconscious enters consciousness—if you let it. Dreams carry messages from the instinctive to the rational part of the mind.

Pay attention to your dreams. You will increasingly find yourself acting in accord with your whole psyche, not just with a piece of it.

How did you feel after the last time you made a big decision?

Dummkopf

Only a dummkopf can call someone else one!
— Peter Urs Bender

Anyone who has ever watched *Hogan's Heroes* on TV knows what the word dummkopf means—a person, usually a guy, who isn't too bright. It's a word that translates perfectly from one language to another.

Often, it's simply "differences" that make a dummkopf. If somebody is different from anyone else, he can become an object of ridicule, hence the term. You'll find that in any family, nation, or maybe even in any religion. Groups that don't think, act, behave, or believe the same way are regarded as dummkopfs.

Even you, my dear reader, are a dummkopf to someone else! Because you are reading a book about Gutfeeling, someone who doesn't believe in it might think you're not too bright.

There's nothing wrong with being a dummkopf, but it's pretty dumb to call others by that name. It's too easy a way out for a bright person to call someone else a "dim-wit."

When did you last call someone a dummkopf? Who was that again?

Ego

Talk to a man about himself and he will listen for hours.
— *Benjamin Disraeli, British statesman*

We all know people with gigantic egos. Their heads are so swelled, they've outgrown the largest hat size available. They talk more about themselves than you can stand to listen to, and they think they are the only ones down here on earth. Me, myself, and I seem to be the only words they know.

Long ago we thought the Earth was flat and the universe revolved around it. Some might still think so. Even though we now know the Earth is just a little speck in nowhere, lots of us still feel that way. We all still strive to be the center of the universe. There's nothing wrong with thinking of yourself as being "at" the center of everything. After all, your view of the world starts with the speck that is you in the universe.

Yet, there is a sense in which we *are* at the centre of the universe without even trying. T.S. Eliot called it the "still point of the turning world." He meant that when you are properly "centered" in yourself, "you" are the point around which the world turns. The real universe starts from within.

Your inner being is the only point from which to understand the universe, however imperfectly. You are part of it.

That's a far cry from the ego that *demands* everything revolve around it.

There is a fine difference between feeling the universe evolves from within and feeling the universe revolves around you. But there's a big difference in the outcome.

When did you last feel in total harmony with everything?

Epitaphs & tombstones

That would be a good thing for them to cut on my tombstone:
Wherever she went, including here,
it was against her better judgment.

— Dorothy Parker, author

Alfred Nobel, the chemist and inventor of dynamite, who established the Nobel Prizes, once read a journalist's account of his life. It had been written on the rumor of his death. In the article he was described solely as a munitions manufacturer. Nobel was so disturbed that he decided he wanted to be remembered as more than the inventor of the most devastating explosive the world had ever seen. He began working to change his image from that of a destroyer to that of a lover of peace.

When he did die, in 1896, he left instructions that the major part of his estate, more than 33 million Swedish Kronor—a staggering fortune at that time—should be used to award annual prizes to those who, in the preceding year, had most benefitted mankind. He selected five major areas of achievement: physics, chemistry, medicine, literature, and peace.

The result? Today Alfred Nobel is remembered as a great humanitarian and philanthropist. The moral? Plant now the seeds by which you want to be remembered.

Epitaphs are like personal mission statements. Those who write them (not just famous people) show by them they are thinking hard about life and death. Such statements highlight the character of the person. What, for instance, would you make of the character of Dorothy Parker, the woman who wrote the epitaph I quote above. Or about the other epitaph she suggested for herself: "Excuse my dust." Yes, she was a poet and humorist. She wanted to be remembered for her tart tongue and sharp words.

And what about the epitaph that William Butler Yeats, one of the great poets of the 20th century, gave himself? "Cast a cold eye on life on death. Horseman, pass by." Whatever else these words do, they set you thinking. And that's what Yeats always wished his audience to do, taking them far beyond the ordinary world through his poetry.

One of the best epitaphs I've ever seen was carved on a stone in an Ontario pioneer cemetery: "He felled the tree, then the tree felled him." Or take movie actress Gloria Swanson's epitaph: "When I die my epitaph should read: 'She Paid the Bills.' That's the story of my private life."

W.C. Fields, never one to depart the stage without a last line, has a classic epitaph: "On the whole, I'd rather be in Philadelphia."

My own will be the titles of my books engraved in stone—so we might sell a few more!

What does this have to do with Gutfeeling or intuition? Simply that if you try to create an epitaph for yourself, and do it honestly, or with your tongue in your cheek, you might not like the picture it leaves of you. Nobel didn't want to be remembered as just a "munitions manufacturer."

To create an epitaph, you have to work at it. That means you have to examine yourself and your life. You may not ever write one you like, but the process will help you to focus on the image others have of you, and the image you want to leave of yourself.

T.S. Eliot said, "We shall not cease from exploration and the end of all our exploring will be to arrive where we started and know the place for the first time."

What words do you want for an epitaph?
How do you want to be remembered?

Executive

Noun. One that exercises executive or managerial control.
—Merriam-Webster Online Dictionary

If you look at your own life, you are the executive of yourself. If you're not happy with the results you get—fire your executives. Change your friends. Change your tactics. But be sure you change something or you'll get the same result as you always had.

Individually you are only one person, but if you look closely you will find many characters in your persona. There is, hopefully, a mother, father, caregiver, driver, lover, friend—you are not just one person, you are a multi-faceted individual. You are also an executive, someone who "manages" the whole "you." If the executive doesn't believe in spirituality, then you yourself won't.

Our Western culture encourages us to live our lives like executives, people making decisions. We are often encouraged to show less emotion and intimacy—to become logical and totally rational.

I'm not encouraging anyone to become a warm, fuzzy, hugging individual. Yet that's part of our makeup. I believe the executive side is the main part of that makeup. But if the executive part of you doesn't believe in spirituality, your other "characters" won't.

Can you imagine working for a president who sees his main task as helping his employees develop to their full potential? Eventually his company would be the beneficiary. You would be astonished at the spirit of cooperation and teamwork in that environment. The president's attitude will permeate his whole corporation. His employees will recognize the new spirit and outperform themselves.

Look at the top executives of any company and analyze their characters. You will discover in them the character of their company. There is an easy way to do this. To check the character of *your* company, visit *www.Bender.ca*, the section under personality analysis, and check yourself out.

As executive of your own being, how do you make your decisions — on logic alone or on emotion as well?
Are you a flexible executive?

Failure

It's hard to fail, but it's worse never to have tried to succeed.
— Theodore Roosevelt, U.S. president

There are some who don't believe in the idea of values at work. They claim to have tried applying them, and failed. It simply didn't work, they say.

Show me the system that works one hundred per cent of the time! Even the great saints and sages of history had their dark moments.

Incidentally, most of these individuals didn't ever think of themselves as saints, sages, or prophets. They felt they were simply students who were trying, and often failing, to understand and apply values and ideals in their lives.

Gutfeeling, instinct, or spirituality may not work every time. Why? Often because people make mistakes. Planes crash. Operations fail, even when techniques are perfect. Planets collide. Meteors fall. Nothing works one hundred per cent of the time.

Yet I think the failure rate of someone who listens to his Gutfeelings, instinct, or spirituality is lower than the rate of someone who does not. Why? Life is like that.

I have to say that if you find a system that works often, or most of the time, you have the best system you can find. Take the approach that everything fails, sooner or later. A failure ratio will always exist. Don't worry about it—but don't give up trying. A little bit of failure is good for you—just please don't make it a habit!

> *Did you stumble recently? Did you struggle to your feet?*
> *Did you regain your composure?*
> *Remember: You fail only when you fail to try again.*

Financial freedom

A lot of money is money you need and don't have.
— Peter Urs Bender

Everyone thinks they're underpaid and overworked. We all aim for financial freedom. But to live a more satisfying life, maybe you should reduce your expectations. You don't have to give up your financial dreams. But be realistic about your earning potential. Look carefully at your actual needs.

There is a story about a high achiever who takes an island holiday in a foreign country. He meets a young boy lazing about the beach. In conversation he tells the lad how important it is to work, to improve his English, to go to university.

When the boy asks why, the tourist replies, "So you'll have money like me to be able to come down here on vacation."

The boy looks at him as if he's crazy and says, "I live here all year round. What more do I need?"

Ask yourself: "What do I really need?" You can't take it with you.
And if you could, the exchange rate would kill you!

Flowers

A wedding is just like a funeral
except that you get to smell your own flowers.
— Grace Hansen, dance director

Remember the flower children? They had good ideas. They were right…and they were wrong. Mostly they were suggesting that it was important to slow down and smell the flowers.

Flowers take time to grow. So does Gutfeeling.

Flowers multiply. So does Gutfeeling, if you allow it to.

Flowers come in their own season. Gutfeeling does, too.

Flowers can be cultivated. Gutfeeling must be.

Flowers need light, water, warmth. Gutfeeling needs belief.

Flowers can be overrun by weeds. So can Gutfeeling.

Flowers can be bought. Gutfeeling has to be home-made.

In a neglected garden, it's not that the flowers stopped growing —
it's that the weeds were allowed to prosper!

Football

Football is an honest game. It's true to life. It's a game about sharing. Football is a team game. So is life.

—*Joe Namath, football star*

Football is a game of strategy. But it's more than that. In many ways it's a metaphor for life. It's a game of physical skill and analysis. Its moves are structured and it follows a system of rules that, once learned, are easily comprehended.

But it's as much a game of Gutfeeling and intuition as any game can ever be. Apart from the fact that football is a male sport, its practitioners exemplify many of the things we're talking about in this book.

It's about leadership, balance, intuition, careful analysis, taking risks. It's about putting your strength and wit on the line. The emphasis is equally on the physical and the mental. Football can be a game of violence. But violence is a fact of life. I don't encourage it, but when it happens, it happens.

Listening to football coaches talk about the game is like reading a manual on how to succeed in life. Famous coach Knute Rockne admits that football is a game of arms, legs, and shoulders—"but mostly from the neck up." Coach Paul Brown sees football as a game of errors, with the team that makes the fewest the winner.

Others see the game as being about life and change. It's about winning and losing with grace. It might seem almost a contradiction in terms, but football stirs those who play it and those who watch it. Spectators admire feats of athletic prowess, but they also compare the game with life and think about consequences.

The writer Lewis Grizzard compares football with "the game of life." "You have to tackle your problems, block your fears, and score your points when you get the opportunity," he says.

Player Jack Kemp says pro football gave him a good perspective on life. "When I entered the political arena, I had already been booed, cheered, cut, sold, traded, and hung in effigy."

Bear Bryant, a famous coach from the last century, had the following advice:

> "If anything goes bad, I did it.
> If anything goes semi-good, then we did it.
> If anything goes real good, then you did it.
> That's all it takes to get people to win football games."

Compare that with my comments about leadership in the section of that name. He understood.

If you participate in a football game, you are immediately aware that though you might know a lot of strategy, it's different on the playing field. There you have to remember the strategy but put it into the back of your mind. Then you open yourself to the play and, in the best of circumstances, let your Gutfeeling take over. Follow the rules but play with spontaneity!

> *Do you enjoy a sport by playing, watching, participating, and seeing it in terms of "the game of life"?*

For men only...

You must train your intuition—you must trust the small voice inside you which tells you exactly what to say, what to decide.

—Ingrid Bergman, movie star

This book would not be complete without some observations on how women make more and better use of intuition. Even today, in the modern world, men are more likely to be raised to pay little attention to their emotions—especially Gutfeeling, intuition, and inner feelings. More and more male managers are able to escape this trap. That says a lot about our society. It is gradually changing—and about time, too!

Women do pay more attention to their emotions than men. They are able to combine their thought processes with their intuitions. They do this, I believe, "instinctively." This is not to say that women are not capable of cold, hard, analytic, so-called "scientific" thinking. But they seem able, even in the midst of tremendous social pressures, to maintain their "Emotional Quotient." And merge it with their modern business thinking.

Are women superior to men when it comes to listening to their Gutfeeling? I would have to answer yes. I also have many male friends who have told me that women managers have given them astonishing insights into the problems they had—especially if there was an emotional dimension to them. In fact, many men have come to rely on the input of female judgement in this area.

Is there a moral here? Yes. If a man is not listening to his Gutfeeling, he would be well advised to take counsel in this area. He should connect with a woman whose judgement he trusts. He will be amazed at the emotional insights the opposite sex can offer. They could be applied to a simple, straightforward business plan. Or a complex merger or two totally different departments or companies. If a man is not too bull-headed, or afraid to take counsel from a woman, he should learn to listen to his female colleagues.

There are many instances in modern business where a woman's words about a business plan have been almost visionary. They see things men do not, and make plans using considerations that are often ignored by males. Part of listening for your own Gutfeeling should be listening to what women have to say about the same things. Don't be afraid! It won't hurt too much!

When was the last time
you really listened to a woman's viewpoint
about your business plan?
Seriously now?

Fortune telling

Change yourself, change your fortunes.
— *Chinese proverb*

Fortune telling is the second oldest profession in the world. We all love to learn what's in store for us, particularly if it's good. Fortune telling is not Gutfeeling, and Gutfeeling is not fortune telling. Yet they are connected.

Carl Jung, in his introduction to his psychological study of the Chinese text of the *I Ching,* known in English as *The Book of Changes,* suggests that the Eastern fortune-telling device is really a means of helping us get in touch with our subconscious. He sees it as a way to "interpret" what I call Gutfeeling.

That's because the book encourages us to action. Telling or "casting" a fortune using the *I Ching* involves drawing yarrow stalks in a certain pattern. (Imagine the "pickup sticks" of your childhood.) Or it may involve casting three coins (think "quarters"). The result is a hexagram, so-called because of its six-line structure. It determines one of sixty-four fortunes which are valid for you at that particular moment. Today, you may even access the *I Ching* on the Internet, or buy a CD program to make it easier.

"At that moment" is an important qualification. It points you in a given direction. But the circumstances of the moment may be valid for only a short time. Using the *I Ching* requires regular casting. You are encouraged to turn to it when you are troubled or when you are genuinely seeking an answer. It's also a subtle way of getting you to regularly review the good, solid advice the book contains.

Jung approves of the book being used in such a manner. Casting your "fortune" using the methods outlined in the *I Ching* is an intensely personal process. It must also be accompanied by some serious personal analysis about how the "fortune" you have "cast" is related to your personal circumstances. It can produce remarkable results when used in this sensible way. But remember that it's only a tool for personal guidance. It comes from an ancient culture that had a lot of practice in codifying guides for behavior. It's a finger pointing the way, nothing more.

Nobody can predict the future or everybody can predict the future. One can guess the future. If out of ten guesses we get eight right, we have become experts. Some people have made a fortune by telling others' fortunes. But if they're so good at it, why didn't they make a fortune on the stock market too?

Gutfeeling may be seen to be a fortune-telling system all on its own. For me the big question is whether one can believe in Gutfeeling and not in fortune telling and vice versa. I think the answer is yes, one can. The reason is simple. Anything you believe is right and real to you. Anything anyone believes is right to him or her. As you believe, so shall it be. Belief determines action.

Just remember: If someone says you have a promising future, believe it. If someone says you have a poor future—deny it! Your best fortune-teller is the one that comes from within.

When did you last read the fortune and leave the cookie?
You might have left the best part!

Geld

I don't like money actually, but it quiets the nerves.
—Joe E. Lewis, comedian

Some people think money is the root of all evil. Geld itself has no character. But too great a desire for it can create evil behavior.

I personally still believe it is better to be rich, young, beautiful, and healthy, than poor, old, ugly, and sick.

You must have heard stories about people who have won lotteries.

Before winning, Joe was miserable. He hated himself, his job, the world. He could hardly be civil to anyone. Suddenly he came into lottery money. He thought his life would change for the better. It did, at least for a year or so. But a few years later he was broke again. The cause was not the money. It was his character. If you hate yourself and your world, nothing will make any difference in your life until you change your way of thinking.

But what about the story of the wealthy industrialist who, on his deathbed, gathered his daughters around him and said, "Soon I'll die. You will inherit all my money. I hope you'll all have as much fun spending it as I did making it."

In our modern world, many are selling their souls for geld. Listen to your Gutfeeling. How much is enough? We all need some. But the more we have the more we seem to need.

Have you ever met a person who says he has too much money?

Golf

Golf is a spiritual game. It's like Zen.
You have to let your mind take over.

— *Amy Strum Alcott, golfer*

All great sports depend on analysis and instinct. Golf does, too.

There's a wonderful story about a rabbi from Israel who was invited to a conference in Florida. As it happened, his room backed onto a golf course. He woke up at 4:00 a.m. After looking carefully around and seeing no one on the course, the rabbi, even though it was the Sabbath, took out his clubs and headed for the fairways.

Above, Moses noted this breach of religious etiquette. He went off to tell God, recommending that the rabbi be punished. God looked down just as the rabbi began his swing, and winked. The rabbi scored a perfect hole-in-one!

Moses protested. "A hole-in-one is punishment?" God just looked at him sadly for a moment, then said, "But Moses. It's the Holy Sabbath. He can't tell anyone about it."

Think of the days, months, and years a golfer practices to get the game perfect! When you watch professional golfers on television or on the course itself, you marvel at the ease with which they play.

Yet each hole in each game requires careful conscious analysis. How far does the ball need to go? Which way is the wind blowing? How strong is it? How hard is the ground? When the ball hits, how far will it bounce? What club is needed? These and dozens of other conscious calculations go into preparing to swing.

But the swing itself is pure Gutfeeling, pure Zen. Sure, it's based on lots of experience, but no matter how much experience a golfer has had, in the end he or she just has to let go! Let go and let instinct, Gutfeeling, and training take over.

And how long does that swing take? A fraction of a second! For that one instant the world stands still and the golfer lets his whole being focus on putting that little white sphere down the fairway and onto the green. That's Gutfeeling at work!

Listening to Gutfeeling doesn't involve holding it close for a long time. Often it just happens in a flash. Your objective is to recognize the instant, the flash, the intuition that makes everything right. Every swing by every golfer on the circuit requires Gutfeeling. But even though it does, is every swing perfect? No.

Gutfeeling itself isn't perfect. Or perhaps I should say that the "feeling" in Gutfeeling is perfect, but the way we engage it might not be. In the words of Robbie Burns, "There's many a slip 'twixt the cup and the lip."

It's possible to be distracted at the instant of the swing. Or to adjust it just slightly so the results are off. But everyone who has watched the pros in action can tell when the golfer's Gutfeeling is right on. There's a "sixth sense" that tells you when a stroke is perfect, when the ball is true. You know you're seeing Gutfeeling in action, even though you may not have thought of it that way before.

Listen to a golfer when hitting a hole-in-one. What's the mood?

Growth

To me, the function and duty of a quality human being is the sincere and honest development of one's potential.

— *Bruce Lee, movie star*

Growth is good. But it may be painful. The emotional pain we have all experienced. Lost job opportunities. Unhappy love affairs. Divorces. Deaths of loved ones. No wonder we call these experiences character building!

And remember all those painful physical growth pains you had when you were young? Teeth growing in, then falling out. Legs growing it seemed about a foot a month? Remember going on your first date—meeting your date's parents? Remember not knowing what to do with your sex urges?

The growth of any company or department is filled with as much pain as it is with joy. Is it any wonder, then, that if you can develop your Gutfeeling, there is a discomfort stage, too?

But looking back, any growth we ever went through left us proud of the end result. We know that as persons we have grown.

What was the most joyful growth pain you have experienced?

Gutfeeling

*A feeling in your body that makes you
stop or go, hold or fold, decide yes or no.*
—Peter Urs Bender

Many individuals think they can't identify Gutfeeling. Even when they have it. I well remember talking to a prominent businessman I had known for some time about Gutfeeling. I asked him if he ever used it in making business decisions. His emphatic reply was "Never!" It was as if he thought he might have been caught with his hand in the till.

"I always make all my business decisions by reason, logic, and analysis," he said. "Then I present the decision to the Board, and we kick it around. If everyone 'feels' the thing seems right, then we proceed."

I asked him what he did when he had finished his reasoned and logical analysis. Did he proceed right away?

"Oh no," he said. "Before I present anything to the Board, I always sleep on it, and after I've presented it to the Board, I ask them to sleep on it and think about it for a few days."

Then he realized he had made an important admission. He went on to admit sheepishly that if he had slept on it and it didn't "feel" right, he didn't proceed with it. And then, more sheepishly still, he allowed as how his Gutfeeling did play a role in his business decision-making. (George Cohon's letter makes the same point at the beginning in this book.)

He had just never thought of it before. Nor had he tried to identify what his Gutfeeling was or where it lay. Most of us are like that. In our world we're just not used to thinking about our emotions or analyzing our "feelings."

> *Making a decision? Ask yourself, "How does it feel?"*
> *That component is your Gutfeeling about it.*

Habits

Habits are cobwebs at first; cables at last.
— Chinese proverb

To establish a new habit takes only a few attempts. Five, according to the experts. After that it's fixed. It's possible to "unfix" it, but that is much more difficult. To break a bad habit or overcome a phobia one has to "undo" the habit at least forty times. The best way is not to fight it, but to establish a new habit in its place.

Provided your habits don't result from addiction, you will find the ability to establish and disestablish them one of the most useful "habits" you can acquire.

Habits are often spoken of in the negative, as in "bad habits." But I believe they are more useful to us than we give them credit for. With the "right" habits, you don't have to think about putting the garbage out every Tuesday night. Or getting the kids ready for school at a certain time. Or getting a haircut every few weeks. Or showing up on time for meetings. Or reading the newspaper for only twenty minutes instead of two hours a day to keep yourself up to date.

I recommend listening to your Gutfeeling as a habit.

First, ask yourself if you have done sufficient analysis of the problem. Then every time you make a decision think, "Is my Gutfeeling telling me anything about this? Do I feel excited about it, or does it make me feel uneasy or nervous?" If you start feeling negative vibes, take a little longer to make the decision. Don't hesitate to take a risk that you recognize as a risk, but don't rush into something you're nervous about. It could prove foolhardy.

If you establish such a habit, you won't have to stop every time and wonder what to do next. Your habit will have prepared the ground for you. Effortlessly you can proceed to the tough stuff.

Have you ever tried to create a habit deliberately?
Try it five times. The system works.

Happiness

Happiness is good health and a bad memory.
— Ingrid Bergman, movie star

Happiness is a belief or a state of mind. It's not a tangible. You cannot buy it. As I see it, the more you run behind happiness, the less you will have.

The ancients knew that certain external conditions are favorable to happy living. Health, beauty, money, and luck (yes luck!). They're all important not because they're good in themselves, but because without them man's nature normally does not get a fair chance to express itself.

I believe the ancients hit the nail on the head. It's pretty difficult to be happy if you are very ill, very ugly, or very poor.

It should be obvious that if you're sick you're not happy. If you're very homely, cross-eyed, unhygienic, and short, it's hard to get others to listen to you. Most of us can't see past the externals.

You need enough money. Remember, a lot of money is any money you need and don't have. Those who are very poor are working hard just to pay the bills. They have no time to read a book like this,

Peter Urs Bender

or even to think about ideals or values.

You need luck, too. It's really chance, or the random factor in life. Just think of your own existence. You're the lucky sperm! At the instant you were conceived, millions raced to fertilize your mother's egg: 9,999,999,999 didn't make it—but you did!

Happiness is a by-product of having done something or of trying to do something. In our world, we tend to believe happiness comes from gathering and getting things or from giving things.

Certain people are blessed with more happiness than others. Life is not fair. Others are given more hair, better looks, deeper voices, and richer relatives.

Real happiness is being happy with yourself. It could come from accomplishing something or from trying to accomplish something. It could also come from pleasing others. It comes from within you.

Lots of cultures don't encourage us to give credit to ourselves. I believe strongly it's your job to give credit to yourself. And also to give credit to those around you.

In Europe, it's the custom to wear lucky stones and charms. There are charms for just about everything a person could want. The ones that sell the most? Money, love, and luck.

What is it that will make you happy tomorrow...
and the day after tomorrow?

Horoscopes

Methods for predicting the future:
1) read horoscopes, tea leaves, tarot cards, or crystal balls...
collectively known as "nutty methods";
2) put well-researched facts into a sophisticated computer...
commonly referred to as "a complete waste of time."

— Scott Adams, cartoonist

Without knowing your birth date, I'm pretty sure I can cast your horoscope. It will convince you I know all about you:

Sometimes you are too honest about your feelings and you reveal too much of yourself. You are good at thinking things through for yourself and you like to see proof before you change your mind about anything.

When you find yourself in a new situation, you are very cautious until you find out what's going on, and then you begin to act with confidence.

Your personality has a few weaknesses but you can generally compensate for them. Sometimes you have difficulty making decisions and you have serious doubts about whether you've done the right thing.

You don't like being told that you can't do something and you become bored when you have to live with too many restrictions because you like a little change and variety in your life.

You are able to discipline yourself so that you seem in control to others, but actually you sometimes feel somewhat insecure. You wish you could be a little more popular and at ease in your interpersonal relationships than you are now.

My colleague and friend John Robert Colombo did the above reading for me—and did it so well he sucked me in completely—80% of it was 100% me. Everyone likes to hear nice things about him or herself, especially from a knowledgeable friend.

To see just how well this works, compare it to the reading below. It's more or less the same, except the meaning of every statement has been reversed. Very few people would say it fits them. However, I bet you have a relative who fits the reading perfectly!

You charge into a new situation before you know what you're doing, but after you find out what's going on you lose confidence in yourself. You make up a lot of stuff about yourself, but you still can't impress people.

You never think for yourself and never change your mind—even when shown proof.

You have a lot of bad personality traits that you never try to overcome. You make snap judgements and never regret it.

You enjoy being told what you can and cannot do by others. You don't like trying new things.

You have no self-control and that makes you feel confident. You seek out people who don't like you, and then insist on spending time with them.

Astrological character readings can be fun, as long as they are viewed as fun. But they can also be harmful if you start to take them seriously. La Rochefoucauld, the 18th-century French statesman, said it best. "Flattery is counterfeit money which, but for vanity, would have no circulation." Watch it!

How did you feel the last time you read a positive, flattering assessment of yourself and your behavior?

Insight

A moment's insight is sometimes worth a life's experience.
— *Oliver Wendell Holmes, philosopher*

Employees with too much insight often drift off-target. They move in circles, and the higher up in the management corps they are, the bigger the circles.

If you know too much about a company, you may become a difficult person. If your coworkers think you know too much they'll see you as someone with the master-key to company secrets that not even the Mounties, Scotland Yard, or the FBI has access to. They'll also become suspicious of you and you may also attract the anger of corporate managers by being too insightful.

To me, insight is a form of self-knowledge. All of the above simply means that if you are insightful, you ought, in general, to keep it to yourself. I respect someone who lives by his or her own beliefs. But I'm always suspicious of those who flaunt their beliefs too openly. Share when asked, but be suspicious of those who come on strong.

Spirituality is the same. Be sure it's inside you. Don't overwhelm others with it, or preach about it, or insist that people know what it is, and seek it hard, too. The way? Be quiet and personal. Let your spirituality show by example, not through empty words.

Tell me when was the last time
you heard two people who were arguing
about their beliefs come to an agreement?

Instinct

Instinct — Animal.
Intuition — Woman.
Logic — Male.
— Anon., 1232 A.D.

When we think of instinct we think of animals and of being pre-programmed from birth. We explain it as the migrating instinct of birds and the survival instincts of animals. There is no question that animals do incredible things by instinct that seem amazing.

But humans are creatures of instinct, too. We don't fall out of bed (most of the time). We breathe even when we sleep. We don't break wind in front of strangers. We digest our food without thinking about it. We do it by instinct. We call it "subconscious behavior."

Instinct and Gutfeeling go hand in hand. What we do by instinct, we do unconsciously. Think of the "fight or flight" response. In humans the response can be so strong we react even without think-ing about it. But sometimes neither fight nor flight responses are appropriate. That's when it most pays to take a step back and con-sciously make a decision.

The more your decisions become conscious, the more appropriate your actions will probably be. Gutfeeling, while intuitive in nature, I see as the subconscious becoming conscious. The more conscious your decisions become, the less you have to worry about an instinctual response getting you into trouble. Try to develop your Gutfeeling. Make more use of it to help enrich your life.

This is not scientific analysis or rocket science. An instinct seems to me to be something one does—through the unconscious. We're not really conscious of it happening. Assuming our unconscious is the force that drives our instincts, we should look into ourselves to see if we have more unknown genes (instincts) which we never use. Can we develop them? I think we can.

How? First we have to agree that what we just discussed here has a point. Then we should trust ourselves to work on it and try it out.

How can you make yourself become conscious of something you used to do on automatic pilot?

Labels

If you change the product's name
it won't change the ingredients.

—Anon.

Labels, or names, can be both empowering and limiting. Simply naming something tends to give it an individual existence. The ancients recognized this connection between names and power.

I use different names for myself when I'm pursuing different activities. I answer to "Benderini" when I run, "Benderstein" when I push myself, and "Bendovani" when I listen to music. Does a name make a difference? Sometimes. Yes.

Yet, in another sense, labels limit understanding. All too often we give something a name, and then think we understand everything about it. For instance, if you start to wear larger sizes you can shop in an expensive, exclusive hoity-toity store. You'll probably pay more, too. But you will also find that you fit into a "smaller" size.

What has this to do with Gutfeeling or spirituality? The labeling of something is an aspect of what we have come to know as "science." Science objectifies, quantifies, labels, and systematizes. Because it can't do that easily with Gutfeeling, it gives the thing a label and dismisses it.

I don't usually quote long passages from other writers, but the following passage struck me as being right on the money. In her book *Thunder Mountain*, novelist Rachel Lee reflects:

> If you couldn't label it and put it in a laboratory, it didn't exist. There was a certain perverted security in dismissing anything that couldn't be precisely quantified. Or in dismissing anything that could be reproduced through quackery. Like that group of scientists who insisted on dismissing paranormal phenomena because the effects could be reproduced by a [stage] magician…never realizing that being able to produce those effects didn't necessarily mean they had found the only means by which they could be reproduced. That was like saying a full-spectrum light bulb produced light the same way the sun did simply because both produced the entire spectrum. When had science become so perverted?…When had it stopped recognizing that it was a search for the real causes behind observable effects, that it was not in the business of dismissing effect because the cause was not apparent.

What Rachel Lee is saying is don't let the labeling of things deceive you. It wasn't done before, but now it's fashion. You have to have a label to be "cool." Names have power, yes, but they are only substitutes for the realities behind them. Look for the reality.

Have you observed others dismissing feelings with labels?
Have you observed yourself
slapping labels on other people?

Leadership

A leader is best when people barely know he exists.
— *Lao Tsu, philosopher*

Leadership is something that can't be learned academically or intellectually. Its principles can be taught, but you can't learn how to lead from a book. Nevertheless, thousands of books have been written about doing so, including one of my own.

If you look at my book *Leadership from Within,* you will see that embedded in the title is the key to all my advice. To study leadership, you need to lead, but you can't lead others until you can lead yourself.

Here is a useful illustration of the two types of leadership: Take a short, three-inch piece of string. Lay it out on the desk in front of you. Then pull it along the desk by one end. You can make it go anywhere and it will follow you. Now try pushing it. The string will pile up and—nothing happens!

Leadership is not about pushing anyone except yourself. But you pull others along if you set a good example. Acting as if you "barely exist" is the way to go. As a leader, you are not there to beat people over the head. Your task is to nudge, encourage, suggest, listen, and empathize. Then, as the philosopher Lao Tsu said in his *Way of Life*, "When your task is done, all the people will say, 'We did this ourselves.'"

A good leader can "sense" how his employees, audiences, or citizens are responding to his requests to turn in a desired direction. Being able to listen to his or her own Gutfeeling is critical to the process. That's why I emphasize the "innerness" of leadership. The more you understand about yourself, the better you will understand others. Gutfeeling plays a major role along the way.

On the battlefield, Napoleon had thousands of tough French soldiers ready to fight for him and give up their lives. But when he came home he had big problems with his wife.

Not much has changed.

Today employees may ask the boss, "How high do you want us to jump?" But in the evening, the boss has to face his spouse.

When did you last meet a leader who led from within?

L eft brain/ right brain

One is right-brained, or left-brained.
Sometimes I feel I'm in the middle: no-brained!

— Peter Urs Bender

The left part of our brain rules the right side of us. Analysis, accounting, logic, and systems are its characteristics. The right side rules the left part. Emotion and intuition, music, art, and poetry come from the right. Gutfeeling comes from the right side of the brain. Then we try to analyze and justify them with the left brain— and often end up throwing Gutfeeling out!

If you are right-brained by nature, you won't have much of a problem getting in touch with your Gutfeeling. It will come naturally. You will still have to work at it, but it won't seem a difficult chore.

If you're left-brained, it's a totally different story. You prefer rational, analytical thinking. As we all know, analysis kills spontaneity. Business people know that too much analysis results in paralysis.

Paralysis by analysis. That's a condition that many modern commentators have observed in fields as different as sports, writing, politics, and business. For individuals, it's a fact that the more analytical you are, the more difficult it is to get "the feeling."

Then, if by some chance you do latch on to a Gutfeeling, your first impulse is to analyze it. Don't! At least not right away. At least not right now.

I suggest that if you're an analytical person, the minute you sense a Gutfeeling, write it down. Forget about it for a while. I must confess that I myself am left-brained by nature. I was trained in the banking and accounting fields. I like to keep track and systematize things.

I never would have been able to write a book like this if I had not trained myself to catch my intuitions on the fly. I make simple notes of them. Eventually I let my left brain have a look at these teasing thoughts and try to organize them. But I don't try too hard. I know if I do I will analyze them out of existence.

I do a fast analysis, then let it go. Then in a week or so I go back and revisit those feelings. I try to let the feelings themselves speak to me. Very few ideas, thoughts, feelings, or intuitions are so good that they cannot be destroyed by logical analysis. The result is "paralysis analysis."

The more analytical you are, the more important this exercise becomes. Joseph Collins, an English novelist, outlined the damaging results of too much emotional analysis. "By starving emotions we become humorless, rigid and stereotyped. By repressing them we become literal, reformatory and holier-than-thou. Encouraged, emotions perfume life; discouraged, they poison it."

Deep inside, as humans, in one way we are all the same. We buy on emotion and justify it with logic.

When did you last buy something over your budget
and later justify it with logic?

Love

And in the end, the love you take is equal to the love you make.
— *Paul McCartney, singer and songwriter*

Falling in love is the ultimate, quintessential Gutfeeling. Everyone (hopefully) experiences it sooner or later. Once you recognize it, you have to agree it does something to you. You feel something somewhere inside yourself. Nobody can explain in words where or what it is. But it is!

If you've never experienced it, you never could explain it. If you have experienced it, you still cannot explain it, but for sure you can feel it.

The experience of love can be overwhelming. That's because it's often the first time we truly feel the tremendous power of emotion. It makes us know ourselves, look at ourselves from within. It comes as a surprise that we are capable of such intensity.

Falling out of love is just as traumatic. It's painful, rather than joyous. If you have experienced it, you will have learned that no emotion can last at such an intense level for long. Love must transcend its original powerful thrust. It must transform itself into something more bearable to live with.

Whatever the case, love makes us recognize depths in ourselves we never knew we had. And whether joyous or painful, the emotion forces us to learn more about our inner selves.

"Falling in love" doesn't necessarily mean with someone of the opposite (or the same) sex. It could be with a job, a house, a car, a country, a city, an animal—many things. It could even be with an idea. There is no logical, analytical explanation of "falling in love." Scientists can only tell us that certain physiological changes take place.

You can feel and sense when you're about to fall in love. At that point you have a choice. You can kill that feeling before it even starts. You can refuse to listen to what is, in fact, your Gutfeeling. Or you can go with the flow.

But you must go one way or the other to experience love. If you wait too long, the feeling will vanish and you are, as the poets say, left "sadder but wiser."

Other Gutfeelings can be controlled the same way. You can encourage or stifle them. Next time you get such a feeling, try to let it happen. Then decide whether to go with it, or walk away from it.

When did you last stop yourself from falling in love?

Lust and greed

A little bit of lust is good for you.

— German proverb

Lust is a form of greed. It is found most often in an economy or environment of scarcity. The question becomes not when is enough enough, but how to get more.

You need a car. Does it have to be a Mercedes? You need new clothes. Do they have to come from Dior or Armani? You need a job. Does your ambition make your desire to reach the top so powerful you will climb over anyone to get there?

We all lust. We are human. The question is, How much attention do we give it?

Writers and speakers like myself are constantly urging their readers and listeners to strive to be excellent. To be the best. To fulfill dreams. Yes, we should have ambition to be the best we can—but not at the cost of everything else. Some people may have to sacrifice more than others to achieve their dreams. But that's not a fault, is it?

The cautionary proverb rings a peal of truth. A little bit of lust helps you to keep your focus. Your focus should be both on others, and on yourself. You need the same things others do. You need to give yourself credit for the things you do. It's not wrong to buy yourself a Mercedes or a Dior. It's wrong only if you can't afford it, or make others suffer for your gain.

Listen to your Gutfeeling. It should tell you when enough is actually enough. Remember, you can't take anything with you.

It's easier to see other people's lust than one's own.
When was the last time you caught yourself lusting?

Manager

*A leader knows what's best to do;
a manager knows merely how best to do it.*

— Ken Adelman, business executive

Jerry White, internationally known business consultant, puts his finger on the critical point of difference between managers and leaders. "Leaders and entrepreneurs use intuition as much as anything in divining vision, strategy and dealing with change. The quantitative bean counters be damned."

Managers follow rulebooks. Good leaders, if they have enough guts, follow their Gutfeeling. Learn to make the distinction yourself.

Rule books are necessary. But all too often they are substitutes for honest reflection and instinct. "Do it by the book" is an expression you will hear all managers use. It relieves them of responsibility for thinking!

There's nothing wrong following the book, unless you are unable to recognize when it's time to set the rule book aside and follow your Gutfeeling. You already have the benefit of the best advice the book can give you. Now forget it, and work out the problem on your own. Let your instincts tell you where to go and what to do.

Keep the book in mind, but don't let it rule in your personal life.

You may work in one of those professions where "the book" is really important, and a certain regimentation is a fact of life. The military, the postal services, the airlines, the railway, the police—all run on manuals. All of these are military or quasi-military operations. "The book" exists to ensure standards of behavior.

It's easy to feel stifled in such organizations. Accept the need for standardization, but don't hesitate to "push the envelope." Even in such companies and services, independent thought, based on Gutfeeling and instinct, is valued, if not always rewarded.

Don't stress the "rightness" of your feelings. But don't fail to express them either. "The book" may not demand it. In fact, it may even inhibit it. But in such organizations, failure to state your reservations can be as damaging as pressing them too hard. Get them on the record. That way you've both satisfied "the book" and salved your conscience. Whether your reservations are acted on or not is not something you can always determine yourself.

If your working environment becomes intolerable, leave it. Don't worry much about your department or even your company. They don't need to declare bankruptcy. They will find a replacement for you. And one day you will be gone anyway.

To keep constantly repressing your instincts is the surest way to become ill. If the atmosphere is so restrictive that you cannot state your feelings without fear of retribution, you're in the wrong job. It's tough to be a leader when the organization demands managers. But you should also respect the fact that certain organizations, by their very nature, require more rigid structures than others. Know it. Don't sweat it.

When was the last time you faced the tough decision to state your Gutfeeling in a hostile environment? What was the result?

Microchips

*The real question is not whether machines think
but whether men do.
The mystery that surrounds a thinking machine
already surrounds a thinking man.*

— B.F. Skinner, psychologist

I'm a great believer in writing things down. If we're not sure of the value of a thought, it often pays to make a note of it. In the old days, we used pads and pieces of paper. Today we can put everything on microchips.

I have a microchip in my car and I record my random thoughts on it from time to time. Once in a while I take it into my office and listen to it. I file those thoughts where I think they belong. I discard those that seem like ramblings. The others are nuggets that I hang on to for reconsideration.

I know that if I don't write things down I'll never remember them all. That has nothing to do with age—I've been good at forgetting things since kindergarten. Great ideas come from Gutfeelings and we'll never know how good they are if we don't write them down and put them to the test.

I had first-hand experience of this recently. On my mother's 80th birthday we had a big party. An uncle she hadn't seen in months came up to her and said, "We must get together. How about next Wednesday at noon?" Mother agreed, then said to me, "Write that down or I'll forget it." I told her not to worry. I'd remember for her. When we got home Mom said to me, "Now when was that meeting I'm supposed to have with your uncle?" My reply, "What meeting? With whom?"

When was the last time you thought,
"What a good idea! I must remember that."
Did you jot it down?
Or is it lost forever?

$\mathbf{M}$iddle

Three Rules of Work:
1. Out of clutter find simplicity.
2. From discord find harmony.
3. In the middle of difficulty lies opportunity.

—Albert Einstein, physicist

"M" is the middle letter of the alphabet. It falls in the middle of the book. You may be in the middle of reading it through. Did you notice changes in yourself? Maybe. Maybe not. That's perfectly normal. It takes a long time to effect change. In my book *Leadership from Within*, there is a graph showing the relationship between Effort and Return.

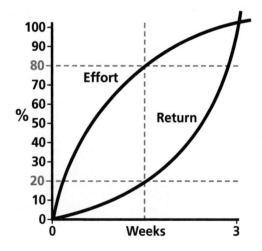

The investment of effort in any project involves much more work at the start than the return might indicate. In fact, halfway through any project, more than 80 percent of your effort has been invested, while you will have reaped less than 20 percent return!

You need to build momentum with any new project. You need to invest more at the beginning than you get out. Your reward or return will come later.

Think about learning to ride a bike. You take baby steps. First you learn to glide with it, then to steer properly. Then things get more complex and you step on the pedals and try to balance. But the most important part is to look where you're going, not down where you are! Eventually you get it!

Learning to identify and trust your Gutfeeling could take as long. The trick is to recognize it first. Don't be discouraged if you can't immediately do it. Keep trying.

It takes a lot of effort to effect a return.
How much effort are you prepared to put into it?

Miracles

*You can either take action, or you can hang back
and hope for a miracle.
Miracles are great, but they are so unpredictable.*

—*Peter F. Drucker, management consultant*

In all religions you will find descriptions of miracles—walking on water, raising the dead, flying on horses, turning water into wine, or even recovering without any losses from disk crashes.

We've all heard of faith healing and prophecy. They are happenings that cannot logically be explained. Did they happen? They must have, because witnesses say they have seen, felt, and experienced them.

But what are they, really? Perhaps they come from a Gutfeeling that changed one's seeing, feeling, or behaving. A miracle can only happen to a person who totally believes it can happen. I personally don't recall a miracle ever happening to me—except maybe that I got the power to quit smoking and lose weight without breaking up my marriage.

There will be moments in your life when things happen you cannot explain. Everyday on television or in the paper you read of individuals who have escaped death by a hair. And every morning when you wake up and there's no tag tied to your toe, in effect it's another miracle. People even describe their escapes or lucky happenings as "miracles," and there is no doubt they seem like that.

There are everyday miracles that give meaning to life. The sunrise every morning. A baby's smile. A lover's caress. A line of poetry that can bring a sudden pang to your heart. But then just to be born is a miracle. To think is a miracle. To stay alive is a miracle. So, maybe, even I myself am a miracle.

As the old saying goes, if you wish to have homemade bread from scratch—you must first create the universe.

When did you last experience a miracle?
(Hint: Don't look for magical events. Look for experiences.)

M ovie

One can see life as a movie. With his tongue in his cheek comedian Steve Martin says of people in difficulty: "You know what your problem is? You haven't seen enough movies—all of life's riddles are answered in the movies." Movies are about imagination and wish-fulfillment.

Remember the saying "Art imitates life"? With movies it seems more that "Life imitates art." English actress Jane Seymour was once heard to comment, "Even though I make those movies, I find myself wishing that more of those magic moments could happen in real life."

Movies are powerful role models. Naturally, given the ability to choose, certain people pick the wrong roles for themselves to imitate. Best is to become the director and assign yourself interesting, big, and powerful roles to play.

In another parallel with life, someone recommends that you see a movie. Yet when you go, you think it's a waste of time. What counts most is that you enjoy the movie and your life!

Movies are made about everything, as Steve Martin's comment suggests. In detective movies, you observe characters frequently acting on hunches.

A hunch is a combination of experience, knowledge, and intuition.

If you can watch and admire the character acting on hunches, what's so difficult about trying to do it for yourself? After all, Gutfeeling doesn't just come from nowhere. It's a result of your own knowledge, experience, and intuition! Give yourself a happy ending.

What's missing in my daily life? The background music from the movies to make it feel more dramatic....

Every movie ends. One day your life will too.
What have you been doing during the run?

Names

The beginning of wisdom is to call things by their right names.
— *Chinese proverb*

What's in a name? It's a question often asked, seldom answered. If names have power (and they do, see Labels) the right name can represent the essence of the thing. The trick with names is not to be seduced into believing they are the thing. They represent essence, not presence.

My assistant George Hancocks tells me as a writer he sometimes becomes "Shannon Moore." It's a name derived from his own various family backgrounds. He says the name can be either male or female. That's because he thinks both "male and female," neither one nor the other, but both in his writing. He also says the name helps him to take a "third-person" attitude and to distance himself from his subject, especially if he's deeply personally involved in it.

When I came to Canada I changed my name. In Switzerland I was known as "Urs Bender." I realized that if I gave Urs as my first name to anyone here the first response would be, "Eh?" So I chose Peter—a perfectly normal North American name, not one that would immediately raise suspicion.

That new name became an important part of my new persona. It made me feel more like a North American. It also allowed me to fit into my surroundings with less difficulty. It also helped me to remember that I was in a different place, under different circumstances, and that I should be a little careful about what I said and where I said it. New culture, new rules.

Names are important to movie stars, too. Peggy Lee was just fourteen when she decided to become a pop singer. Four years later she had changed her name from Norma Engstrom and moved to Hollywood. Do you think such hits as "Is That All There Is?" or "Fever" would have become so identified with her original name? And what about the immortal Marilyn Monroe? Her original name was Norma Jean Mortenson. Can you imagine Rock Hudson as Roy Scherer, Jr.? Or John Wayne, the Duke, the perfect symbol of the raw, rugged, wild west—as Marion Morison?

Here are a few other interesting examples of how critical names can be to success.

Lady Chatterley's Lover, a book title that has passed into legend with time, was originally called *John Thomas and Lady Jane*. John Thomas reminds me of a little boy's first name for his penis. And Lady Jane immediately calls to mind Tarzan's wife. What's in a name, indeed!

And did you know that *Tomorrow Is Another Day* was the original title of *Gone With The Wind*? That Scarlett O'Hara was originally named Pansy? Can you imagine Clark Gable, the greatest romantic movie lover of all time, saying, "Frankly, my dear, I don't give a damn!" to Pansy O'Hara? That immortal parting line to a girl named Pansy would have been like whipping a puppy. Some things were just not meant to be! The big question is when, how, and why did they listen to their Gutfeeling about names.

My own personal favorite is *The Great Gatsby*. Can't you just see Edward G. Robinson with his cigar clamped in his teeth in that title? The book's original name was *Trimalchio in West Egg*. Do you think the new name made a difference?

So don't be afraid to give yourself a new first name. Make it something strong and rich. A new name signals a new beginning. If you're planning on making a big change in your life, change your name. It may make all the difference to the way you approach life.

Do you know anyone who has changed a name?
Did you ever think of changing your name?

Nanoseconds

We divide time into smaller and smaller segments
as if to punish ourselves for being unable to control it.
You can't make time do anything.
You can only use it effectively—because it's all relative.

—*Shannon Moore, writer*

No one is given more time than anyone else. But certain people accomplish far more than others during the same time. It could be that those who accomplish more do it by instinct. Or maybe they just choose to work on more important tasks. It could also be they took time-management training and learned to prioritize the important tasks. The end result is the same. He or she who works on important tasks will accomplish more than he or she who is always running with a bucket of water to put out the fires.

	URGENT	NOT URGENT
IMPORTANT	Things forgotten Deadlines due overdue Crises	*Planning* *Relationships* *Prospecting* *Marketing* *Exercizing*
NOT IMPORTANT	Incoming phone calls Unimportant meetings	Time wasters Personal phone calls Shopping

Gutfeeling can be replaced by a systematic approach to life. But when Michelangelo sculpted David out of marble, did he do it by Gutfeeling or by using a system? We can't say for sure, but we know he did both. He had the creative urge (Gutfeeling). But he couldn't carve the marble without training and a system.

Turn the nanosecond into the macrosecond by using it intelligently and intuitively.

If you had twice as much time today,
would you accomplish twice as much?

Negotiation

Anything is negotiable.
— The Godfather

As a kid, you started negotiating with your parents. How long could you cry until your demands were met? And that was just the beginning! We all negotiate all our lives.

Certain people negotiate better. They aim for more than others. Remember. You don't get what you deserve. You get what you negotiate for.

I am willing to buy your present car for $80,000. The terms are $1 down and $1 per year for the balance. Offer sounds great. But payment terms are lousy and unacceptable.

You have to learn to negotiate with yourself, too. You need to convince yourself to listen more closely to Gutfeeling. Learn to negotiate with yourself after analyzing and scrutinizing. Then listen.

There's a lot of similarity between negotiating and Gutfeeling.

You have Gutfeelings from the very beginning of your life. You negotiate from the moment you're born. You may be able to ignore your Gutfeeling, but you can't ignore the necessity to negotiate.

Negotiating with yourself is simple. Pose a question. Then try to answer it in your mind. If you're not sure you're hearing the answer, force yourself to write one down. You will quickly see whether or not you're answering the questions you posed.

I also find that it helps to write down the questions. Then consciously try to answer them. Consider whether the answer has a positive or a negative effect on you. Try to be honest in grading your answers.

After a while you'll find this mental dialogue comes naturally. You may soon be able to dispense with the written list entirely. But I find that having a permanent record is a good way to check progress.

Some of your answers may surprise you. Writing them down can give you a good handle on where you're coming from.

Consciously try to get in touch with your Gutfeeling when you question yourself. Don't frame your questions in a preconceived way. Answer them unconsciously, spontaneously. Respond the way you might to an ink-blot test or to a personality analysis quiz.

The whole purpose is to bring your Gutfeeling to bear in negotiation. Spontaneous answers will draw out far more information about yourself and your intuition than long, drawn-out, carefully considered replies.

The time for that kind of thinking is later. Once you have the "flash" answers, you can consider them more carefully. Then modify them to suit your circumstances.

What will you negotiate for yourself, with yourself, for today?

Nightmares

Anything not controllable is a nightmare.
— Peter Urs Bender

Something has taken over. In a dream you may feel yourself flee-ing in panic or suffocating. Or you may feel frozen and unable to escape an unbearable situation. Or you may repeat the same useless actions again and again in an endless loop.

Maybe you are walking naked through your department and your best prospect is waiting for you in the office when you get in. Or the boss walks in and catches you making love to his successor on the office floor. Make up your own nightmare. It all comes from within.

Some experience these feelings in the waking nightmares we call phobias. There is a treatment for them. It requires familiarizing yourself with the thing you most fear in a non-threatening envi-ronment. It helps to have plenty of encouragement from a doctor or from someone you love.

Many things in life are uncontrollable. They can create the suffo-cating terror of a nightmare. The traffic. The weather. The state of the economy. Life's most embarrassing moments. None of us have much control over any of them. The trick is to learn to face these nightmares without panic.

Whenever the traffic is bad, for instance, I try to avoid it at any cost. Otherwise, I try to find someone to drive me. I don't get excited as a passenger. If the weather is truly bad or totally unpredictable, I try to avoid travelling completely. Bad weather is a killer.

With nightmares you almost always have a choice. You can accept that you're being drawn into one. Or you can choose not to be involved. Remember. We always have more control over our own four walls than we think.

All through this book I've been urging you to pay attention to your Gutfeeling. But there is such a thing as over-reliance on instinct.

Those who think they can rely on Gutfeeling alone are in a runaway mode and in reality are creating nightmares for themselves. I regard this as the negative aspect of Gutfeeling.

For these individuals, superstitions and seemingly intuitive events have become their reality. Approaching life in this manner is as bad as thinking one can rationalize everything.

Life is a balance. Try for the Middle Way!

When did your emotions last take total control over your feelings?

Options

The strongest principle of growth lies in human choice.
— *George Eliot, novelist*

You might remember this experiment from your school days. Two groups were asked to mentally add up figures in a very loud and noisy environment. One group was given the choice of a button that could eliminate the sounds, but they were asked to use it only if the noises became unbearable. The other group had no button.

The result? The group that had the button but didn't use it added more numbers more correctly than the group that had no button.

What does that tell you? It really says that as long as you think you have a choice, you really do perform better. It doesn't matter who you are or where you come from.

There are times when you think you have no options. Individuals with young families are particularly vulnerable. Raising a family is a task that demands total attention from you and your spouse, all the time. There seems to be no letup. And then somebody says, "Enjoy them. They are only so little for such a small time." But if you have the option that the situation won't last forever, you will perform better.

Use your Gutfeeling as an optional helper to increase your chances of making more right decisions. When you make a big decision, think of your options. Try writing them down. The simple writing process helps to make your options more conscious, and therefore easier to deal with. You may even discover options that didn't occur to you at first. The process of making your Gutfeelings more conscious is a great idea generator. All the information is within you, just ready to pop out if given the right conditions.

Last time you were in a very uncomfortable situation
did you try to analyze all your options?

Power

Power's twin is responsibility.
—Willa Gibbs, writer

Power is all around us. It surrounds us. We possess it. There are some who say there is no such thing as Spiritual Power. They are mistaken. It can heal or harm. Go to any hospital and see. Miracles do happen. Ask physicians. They have experiences with patients they cannot explain.

Yet many negative things have been said about power. It is hard for us even to view it as an aspect of Gutfeeling. Yet power sets our boundaries. It gives form to our relationships. It even determines how much we let ourselves liberate and express aspects of the unconscious.

If something can be described as negative spirituality or Gutfeeling, the naked pursuit of power must surely be it.

But why? Power is not negative or destructive in and of itself. I think it's simply because of the way we end up using it. Or as it ends up using us. The saying is that power corrupts, absolute power corrupts absolutely. It's related to the fact that the *pursuit* of power is a form of greed.

The greed for power can corrupt even the strongest person's spirituality. Yet the fact remains that power is an aspect of Gutfeeling.

In our search for greater spiritual consciousness, we acquire a sort of power. Once we realize what's happening, we're eager for more. That's the time for what I call a "reality check." In my book *Leadership From Within* I have a section on checking progress and results. It applies here.

Look for feedback on the state of your health, your feelings, your relationships, your organizations, the state of your nature. If you're on the right track, you'll feel good about yourself, and you should. If things seem to be going wrong, the "reality check" will give you a warning before things get too out of hand.

Former U.K. Prime Minister Margaret Thatcher used to say that being powerful is like being a lady. If you have to tell people you are, you aren't.

Is your spiritual power expanding? How well are you using it?

Practice

Practice does not make perfect. It simply reinforces behavior.
— Peter Urs Bender

Learning new ways of doing things is difficult at first. If we proceed alone, chances are we may end up creating bad habits. Ask anyone who is getting good at a sport or anything else about the secret. Get a coach. The coach's number-one problem, if you started without one, is retraining your bad habits.

No one yet knows exactly how we learn. Everyone does it differently because we're all different. One thing is for sure. Whatever we practice for long goes into our unconscious.

For instance, if you learn to drive on the right side of the road, then take the opportunity to visit a country where motorists drive on the left. You'll discover you'll get very tired because you have to concentrate so much on your driving. In other words, most of what we do is done automatically because we have programmed ourselves to do it this way.

There are very successful business people who analyze and scrutinize situations then listen to their Gutfeelings. Yet in our society Gutfeeling is suspect. Where did they learn this skill? It was not attending Gutfeeling 101! It would be helpful to have a course like that. The best thing about it is that no one would fail!

I believe these people have great confidence in themselves. They have made many decisions that turned out positively. Gutfeeling is not a fix-all. You can have a positive Gutfeeling and make a wrong decision. Nothing is ever perfect. That's life, and life is not fair!

When was the last time you broke a
long-standing pattern of behavior?
Do you remember what it felt like?

Prejudice

I am free of all prejudice. I hate everyone equally.
— W. C. Fields, comedian

Prejudices are nasty little habits that we form without thinking. The dictionary defines them as opinions "formed without just grounds or sufficient information." We let them happen. Then we let them linger in our unconscious. We rarely pull them out and examine them. They rarely emerge into the light of conscious thought (where we might be embarrassed by them). If they do emerge, it's probably behind the back of a hand whispered into someone's ear. "Look at her. She's a ...." Or "Look at him. Isn't he strange? He must be a ...."

Prejudices are first learned, passed down through generations. Created and reinforced by peer groups. Then they become automatic. From our subconscious they determine the direction of our actions by default.

We are prejudiced against those people who disagree with us. We form a prejudice against anyone who slights us. And how about those who are "different" from us in whatever way? Northerners from Southerners. Ethnic Albanians from Serbians. Tutsis from Hutus. All it takes is three or four repetitions and the prejudice is formed (*see also* Habits). Unless we work at eliminating them, our prejudices are likely formed forever.

When these major prejudices emerge, they cause wars, terrible atrocities, and great anguish. They are often not diminished even when the immediate conflict is over.

So how do we cope with prejudices if we wish to overcome them? I believe we do it the same way I've been advising you to get in touch with your Gutfeeling.

Prejudices can be viewed as "negative" Gutfeeling. What we must do is bring them from the unconscious into the conscious. When we see them, we can deal with them. If we want to!

For instance, every time you catch yourself saying something like "All cab drivers drive like idiots" or "These people don't know how to behave," ask yourself who you mean.

Maybe a cab driver went too fast and nearly knocked you over when he stopped. Do all cab drivers do that? Is it fair to take the failings of one and apply them to the group?

When you refer to "these people," who do you mean? You probably only mean one or a few individuals in a clan, group, tribe, or nationality who has done something or acted in some way you don't like. Is everyone to be tarred with the same brush?

The transference of the "particular" to the "general" is at the root of most prejudice. Learn to recognize when it's happening. If you can't overcome it, at least be prepared to confront it. Try to suspend or redirect the emotion it raises in you.

Who is prejudiced against you?
Or do you think you're the only person in the world
to be prejudiced against a group?

Presentations

Worst Human Fears:
1. Speaking in front of a group
2. Dying
3. Speaking and dying in front of a group

— Peter Urs Bender

It's natural for any presenter to be nervous when starting. When you're green you grow. When you're ripe you rot. So it's good to be a little green. The secret is that no one should see you're nervous.

There are many books that can help you. My first book, *Secrets of Power Presentations*, is now required reading in many companies, colleges, and universities. It has been translated into more than a dozen languages. That's because it's simple, understandable, and easy to follow.

To be more powerful in front of a group when you start, speak twice as slowly as you feel you would like to. Use lots of pauses. This creates curiosity in your listeners' minds, and forces them to listen. Use half as many words as you thought you would need. Remember to smile once in a while, even if the audience looks like they have come from a funeral, or are ready to sit through one.

And remember. It doesn't matter who you are, you always do three speeches. One you prepare, one you deliver, and one you go through on the way home. (The best one is the last one!)

Be sure you prepare an interesting opening and a powerful close. Make these short and precise. Write them out and memorize them. These are the only two sections of your speech you should prepare word for word. But when you're in front of your group and you suddenly get an inspiration, follow your Gutfeeling. Don't use your prepared close. Let your emotion and enthusiasm loose and leave your audience dazzled.

If the last speaker you heard moved you,
did he or she do it with facts? Or with emotion?

Profit

*Also known as net income, profit is
the sum remaining after all expenses have been met or deducted;
synonymous with net earnings and with net profit or net loss
(depending on whether the figure is positive or negative).*

—Jerry White, business consultant

Profit is not a four-letter word. It's six. And without profit, or gain, we have to close the show.

Everything in the universe runs on the profit system. If a church, synagogue, or temple wants to stay in business it needs more new souls. That can be considered the "profit" on its work. No profit. No show. There are commentators today who are afraid this is happening. A church, just like a business, must downsize if it's not keeping its members.

Most of us go to work to bring home a livelihood. If you're smart enough to keep something of what you earned, you can say you've "shown a net profit." I have never yet met anyone who was underworked and overpaid. Yet I have discovered that a lot of people who earn a lot of money are in a lot of debt.

I see spirituality as the unconscious becoming conscious. The more "profitable" the unconscious can become, the more assets our conscious will have. Our objective should be to make the conscious more aware of the unconscious, to all up anything we need with the flick of a thought. The objective is to awaken the unconscious. (Who would want to walk around with all it contains in the forefront of conscious mind!) Think of it as a magical storehouse for all that makes us human. We carry it with us wherever we go. But we need to be able to access it at will.

It only causes us problems when we can't hear it, or worse, when we refuse to listen to it. The unconscious is a remarkable warehouse. It will accept anything we give it, as well as much we don't intend it to retain, but which it does, anyway. It's the parts of us that we don't like to recall. We don't want to "make conscious," or even think about the stuff it contains. That stuff can sometimes cause stress so great it can make us physically ill.

The great Russian writer Boris Pasternak in one of his books likens adolescence to our unconscious and says that "we, like learner airplanes, return to it again and again for petrol."

That's not a bad analogy. As long as we can return to our unconscious (our gut) at will, to "feel" things out and explore them consciously, we're okay. The unconscious carries the "profit" of our life. When we repress it we can turn that "profit" into a "loss."

When did you last add a profit to yourself and to your society?

Quality

ISO 9992.99
Standards have changed.
— International Standards Organization

Quality is about value and excellence. Value is the worth of something, a fair return, a monetary price. Excellence means outstanding, first-rate, tops in its class. Quality control is about measuring the way in which value and excellence are judged. And standards *have* changed.

Ninety-nine per cent is not good enough any more. A study by the Quality Control Institute of California determines that if we are satisfied with 99.9% accuracy, 22,000 checks would be cashed by the wrong bank every hour; 500 incorrect surgical operations would take place each week; 20,000 drug prescriptions would be incorrectly filled each year.

The business definition of quality control is that it is "the process of assuring that products are made to consistently high standards of quality. Inspection of goods at various points in their manufacture by either a person or a machine is usually an important part of the quality control process." It's an effort to ensure that true value and excellence are available to everyone.

It's no different in our progress to spirituality. Quality control for that journey really takes the form of a "reality check" every so often. We need to examine, and then re-examine, our beliefs. If they're based on solid evidence, we retain them and continue to build on the base we've created.

But every once in a while, something questionable, or even down-right incorrect, creeps into our belief system. That's when the reality check, the quality-control examination, becomes critical. It will catch those beliefs and hopefully modify or eliminate them. Prejudices and racism are just two examples of beliefs that creep in. They're hard to modify.

Perform the quality-control examination. Don't let such thoughts contaminate your hard-won belief system.

Have you performed the quality-control exercise lately?
Don't let a thought off your mental assembly line
until you're satisfied it's as close to perfection
as you can make it.

Quorum

Quorum, n.
A sufficient number of members of a deliberative body
to have their own way and their own way of having it.

—Ambrose Bierce, author

Do you ever have the feeling that different instincts are telling you to do two or more different things at the same time? If so, you have become a committee of one. You need to create a quorum to proceed. No board meeting can start anywhere until you have a sufficient number of attendees.

A quorum need not apply just to a business committee. It also applies to a family or to an association meeting.

To punish yourself on earth, you must volunteer for a board or committee. You will quickly see how a group can waste a heck of a lot of time and a huge amount of money. And accomplish nothing.

At the same time, look at companies or associations that grow. They get better. Offer better service to members. There you will find committees whose members are working in harmony to help others.

As individuals we run our own board meetings. In the morning, when we wake up, we meet with ourselves. In the evening, before we fall asleep, we meet again. Whenever we make a decision, we have another one-person meeting.

If we have too many inputs, we become confused. When instincts pull us in different directions, apply the quorum principle. This will help us to go in a direction. Most of the time it will prove to be the right one.

But there is no 100% guarantee. The shortcut to failure is paved with wrong decisions. The long way to failure is paved with no decisions.

When did you last not make a decision
because you had too many mixed feelings?

Rainmaker

If ya don't believe in rainmakers
what DO ya believe in, mistah? Dyin' cattle?

— *Billy Starbuck, in the movie* **The Rainmaker**

The rainmaker is a person whose influence can initiate progress or ensure success. It's meaning has become associated with that of "achiever." The name alone sounds mysterious.

Thousands of years ago the rainmaker was a very important figure, perhaps a witch doctor. Through ritual it was thought he could call down rain to end drought or to ensure rich crops.

In the modern world, he or she may be a scientist, a figure in the stock market, or an important political party member. In science, a rainmaker is actually someone who studies the weather and is able to predict when conditions are right to "seed" clouds and bring forth rain. In the stock market, he or she brings new business to brokerage houses. In politics, the rainmaker is the party's "bagman," bringing in contributions to keep the party solvent. Even the word "solvent" reflects "liquidity." And money, to a party, is rain!

The rainmaker operates on a Gutfeeling level much of the time. Even in science, the ability to cause precipitation is based partly on instinct and hunch.

And what is more intuition-based than politics or the stock market? Both involve a lot of observation and research. But in the final analysis, politicians rely on Gutfeeling to "encourage success."

My point? There are scientists, executives, and managers in our society for whom reliance on Gutfeeling is second nature. They don't talk about it. They don't document it. But ask them how they arrive at their conclusions. They will admit there is always an unknown component.

Think of yourself as your own rainmaker. Perform whatever rituals or stately dances are important to keep you in touch with your own Gutfeeling.

Who is the rainmaker in your world?
How well are you performing the rain dance?

Rebirth

*For now we see through a glass darkly;
but then face-to-face: now I know in part;
but then shall I know even as also I am known.*

—St. Paul, apostle

We live in a universe that is constantly recycling itself in a system of birth, death, and rebirth. Nothing is really new. Everything was here before. Every once in a while it's repackaged.

To me, rebirth is not the physical resurrection of the body on a mythical Judgement Day. It means seeing things clearer in the here and now. The whole thrust of this book is to urge you to take the responsibility for rekindling your Gutfeeling: to begin to see things differently.

How can we not?

We often speak of rebirth as "seeing the light." In cartoons and instruction manuals an idea is often represented as a candle being lit or a light bulb being suddenly turned on. It's a very apt analogy. It's a little like suddenly seeing a new and different view of the world. One modern writer, Albert Camus, called it the "Absurd." When the world turns upside-down and what seemed right before now seems wrong and vice-versa, you've come face-to-face with the Absurd.

True rebirth happens when we are, possibly suddenly and maybe even painfully, called upon to re-examine all our beliefs. If we do it honestly we will wind up seeing things clearer than ever before. I call it the "Eureka Factor" or "The Breakthrough Factor." It owes a lot to our Gutfeeling or intuition.

If you feel you have found the light at the end of the tunnel (and you know it's not a train) you will act as if reborn. Life doesn't change. You do. Your worldview has become clearer.

When did you last experience the "feeling"
of finding something new
or seeing the world through newly opened eyes?

Religion

We have just enough religion to make us hate,
but not enough to make us love one another.

—Jonathan Swift, satirist

All religions would be wonderful—if only people would live and act as their religions encouraged them to do—instead of just bragging about participating in ritual and forcing others to join them. Let me quote G.K. Chesterton: "The Christian ideal has not been tried and found wanting. It has been found difficult; and left untried." And that great commentator on the modern world, Karl Marx: "Religion is the opium of the people."

Religion has been blamed for having done more harm to civilization than it has good. But it has also helped many to live lives that are straight, clean, and powerful, whether as Buddhists, Muslims, Hindus, Jews, or Christians.

Whatever religion you are involved in has dealt with some of the fundamental problems of living. Religion also created the Devil or the Destroyer, clarifying the Gutfeeling we have about certain things that make us uneasy. The very existence of the Devil figure in religion indicates than mankind has always been aware there is a negative aspect to spirituality.

Today we might call that feeling "angst" or "spiritual fear."

Whatever your feelings on the matter of religion—for or against—try not to let them interfere with your attempt to "grow" your own intuition. In fact, if you follow both your instincts and your chosen religion, it might even help you to increase your spirituality faster than if you are not religiously inclined.

But beware of the fact that religion is a great institutionalizer. Institutions, while necessary, tend to inhibit thought. Think like Robert Louis Stevenson: "Every man is his own Doctor of Divinity in the last resort."

How much time have you spent lately finding good things to say about another's religion?

Responsibility

What we need most today is to assume responsibility for our own actions. As well as our own thoughts. Just getting older doesn't mean one gets more mature or responsible. Hair falls out. Joints fail. Sex life decreases. But egos grow larger. Age tends to lend them credibility, even if there's nothing there. Age is mandatory—maturity is optional.

Take responsibility for your actions. Take responsibility for your thinking. Be ready to act. Stop passing the buck for your failure to your parents, teachers, rabbis, monks, priests, imams, ministers, spouses, lovers, partners, or governments. We have inner resources to work with. Think of your sense of humor, your sense of honor, your loyalty to friends, family, and workplace. Think of your capacity to sympathize and empathize with others.

A sense of responsibility can even break up a marriage. They got divorced over religious differences—he thought he was God; she didn't, and moved out.

Don't blame your Gutfeeling if you make a wrong decision. Listen to yourself as if you were the judge on a case. Imagine a social worker hearing a client's plea. Or a parent listening to a child's problem. You hold the responsibility for your life in your own hands. Nobody ever hears both sides of an argument—except your neighbors.

Responsibility starts from within. With you. Not with someone else. Seek out responsible friends and associates. Combine your strengths. Give yourself a place to stand and move the world! Responsible people are needed to manage families, work at jobs, or run businesses. Self-examination on a regular basis is fundamental to the nature of responsible people. Only those who are used to looking for, and listening to, their Gutfeeling need apply!

When did you last notice that
responsibility and inner peace
go hand-in-hand?

Revenge

If you dig a grave for revenge, be sure you dig two.
— Chinese proverb

We have positive and negative thoughts. The positive ones create tons of energy. Negative ones drain us slowly but surely. They can even kill.

Let's face it. Life isn't fair. No matter who you are, at one time or another you will be unjustly treated. When that happens, your back goes up and you start to yell and scream. The desire for revenge becomes almost overwhelming.

You're burning energy, depleting yourself, reducing your concentration. You can even feel it physically. For a while you can sustain the rage and resentment. But then you can slowly feel yourself deflating. The energy level of your emotional battery is draining.

I'm not any different from anyone else. If someone treats me badly, I get upset and react. I have pet peeves just like you that act as emotional buttons. If someone pushes one, I can feel my reaction almost automatically beginning to occur.

I admit that once in a while it's worthwhile to yell and scream and put on a show. But you should be in conscious mode when you do it. Ask yourself, "If I don't protest, will they do it again?" Then adjust your protest to the situation. If it's something minor, forget it. If it's important, consider your response. That's okay. You're still in control, even if the action isn't pleasant.

But there are difficult situations that occur in business. Think of a company going bankrupt. No matter how much of an emotional display you put on, screaming won't make it better. There's only one way to deal with it. Fold the cards and forget about it. Move on. If you hang on to it, think about it, worry over it, the situation will only get worse.

I make it perfectly clear. It's easy to talk—difficult to do. When I'm in those kinds of situations I also often hang on too long. I recognize that. I try to overcome that feeling in myself.

Think about this. If you're in a situation where you've been nailed or victimized, chances are you had some warning. Your Gutfeeling probably gave you some hints that things were shaky. Did you listen to your feeling? Don't let your greed overcome your Gutfeeling.

When was the last time you rehashed
the bad events of your business or social life?
What did the replay do for you?

ROI

Know when to hold them,
Know when to fold them.

—*Las Vegas popular saying*

Sometimes there is *no* Return on Investment. Have you ever had that feeling? You can work and work and work—and in the end you get no or very little return. Time to cut your losses!

Does that mean you should not have invested the time? Maybe. Or maybe not. It all depends!

Sometimes you invest a lot of time in something and it simply doesn't work. Is it time wasted? In one sense yes. In another, no.

Yes, it's time wasted. You could have been going in another direction. You could have invested your time more wisely.

No, it's not totally wasted. You'll know enough not to venture down that path again. That will probably save you from investing time uselessly. Doing the same thing over and over with no return is a waste.

When I speak of Return on Investment in life, I am using a business term metaphorically. Your "investment" is your life. The "return" on your investment is what you make of it. It's impossible to realize your maximum potential without Gutfeeling.

It was in the Silicon Valley. Three project managers in a high-tech company were given money, each according to the importance of the position. One received $5,000, another $2,000, and the third $1,000. Then the boss left on a long overseas journey, telling the group to do what they could with the money.

The first one took his $5,000 and made another $5,000. The second took the $2,000 and made another $2,000. The third manager, using the well-known CYA principle (cover your ass), was afraid of totally losing his $1,000. So he buried it. (This gave rise to the saying "Don't hide your talents under a bushel.")

When the head honcho returned, the first two proudly recounted the success of their investments. He was so pleased he gave them the earned money and promoted them to more important positions.

The third manager, however, using words we'd recognize today, tried to blame the boss for his own lack of success. He simply gave the money back, without even accrued interest. Furious, the boss split the money between the other two, then dismissed the manager "for cause."

To read the original story, go to *Matthew* 25. It talks about Return on Investment.

It's the same with Gutfeeling. The more you have, the more you can get. The more you open yourself to your instinctive nature, the greater will be your return. Your investment is your life. Your return on investment comes through Gutfeeling.

How would you rate your ROI? Does it equal or exceed investment?

Schadenfreude

If something bad happens to you, tough luck!
If something bad happens to me, totally unfair!
If something bad happens to someone I hate — Wunderbar!

— Peter Urs Bender

Schadenfreude means malicious glee. Have you ever felt it? If your answer is "No" you're lying! You're one of those who has never had a spot on their underpants!

You have tried for years to tell your company how important a website is for a contemporary business. Everyone ignores you. In disgust you seek another job. Later, you hear your old company has foundered. Experts suggest its attitude to new technology is at least one reason. How do you feel? Smug is too soft a word. "Hallelujah, I was right!" is closer to the truth. You've just experienced Schadenfreude.

The emotion is often seen as somewhat distasteful and unpleasant. It's generally thought "not nice" to enjoy the misfortune of others. While that might be morally true, we are all human.

Schadenfreude has its place, especially when we feel we have been mistreated or victimized. How often have you heard family or friends in a court case saying they felt "vindicated" by a harsh judgement handed down if the damage to them has been severe?

Victims have a perfect right to experience Schadenfreude.

I believe it's a form of Gutfeeling. But this is a feeling you should-n't actively seek out. If you experience it, enjoy it momentarily. If you have suffered hurt from an individual, association, or compa-ny, you would be less than honest if you did not experience it. But don't hold on to the feeling. That smacks of revenge. Remember, if you're digging a grave for revenge, dig two—one for yourself.

Of course, experiencing Schadenfreude can give you a clue about Gutfeeling itself. It is, after all, an instinctive, intuitive reaction. Where there is one such feeling—there may be more. Look and lis-ten for them.

Does a little Schadenfreude make you feel good?
Does a lot make you feel bad?
What does that teach you about yourself?

Schmutz

Schmutz is a German word for dirt. The English word is remarkably similar. Smuts. Little black flecks of greasy dirt that fall from the air and mark everything.

It's hard to see your own dirt. The inside of a car gets dirty, slowly. Kitchen floors, office drawers, computer files accumulate junk. It doesn't happen overnight.

Everybody has some Schmutz in his life. There's no escaping it. A friend of mine has a mother whose favorite saying is "You have to eat a peck of dirt before you die."

If you move into a new home, you make a mental list of changes you want. For instance, you may notice a cracked baseboard or an appliance knob missing. It bothers you. But you may never get around to fixing them. As time passes, you grow used to things as they are.

Schmutz accumulates slowly around us. After a while we don't notice it. It just grows.

Gutfeeling may be disappearing from us. We might not feel it any more. The more analytical our society becomes, the less we rely on Gutfeeling. Yet we need it to balance our lives.

The quintessential question is:
Are you ready to rekindle your Gutfeeling?

Self-confidence

To get a pat on the back, give yourself a pat on the back.
— Peter Urs Bender

Anyone who can walk and talk—already should have some self-confidence. Think about it. We all start up with nothing. We all have to learn the basics of life. And these very essentials also seem to give us confidence. If we are blessed with the right parents, muscles, schooling, and good looks, we have an advantage.

There is no question that if your spouse or friends tell you how good you are, or how well you look, you get a burst of energy from their faith in you. But don't depend on that pat on the back.

We alone are responsible for our self-confidence. We won't get it from anybody on a regular basis. In our dreams we might get it from our spouse, boss, associates, friends, whomever. It's even good, once in a while, to have moment of self-doubt.

In real life, everybody has ups and downs. The secret is to maintain a careful balance. To believe in yourself. The more self-confidence you have, the more you can trust your Gutfeeling.

When did you help someone else to gain more self-confidence?

Success

*Street smarts can replace education,
but education can't replace street smarts.*

— Seymour Schulich, businessman

Success is both measurable and immeasurable. It can come in many forms—social, self-esteem, artistic, financial. We all have the same brain mass, 1,200 cubic centimeters of it. Most research shows we use only about five percent of its capacity. Many are scared to use even that much, in case it would be non-replaceable!

Successful individuals don't have more brain mass than unsuccessful ones. But they do things differently. They calculate the odds. They don't waste time on trivia. They learn from experience.

It's common to say that success is bred from anguish and pain. Maybe some pain sets us thinking about how to do things better. But mostly pain is pain. It's hard to think, let alone succeed, when you're in agony. Either physical or mental. Success is not so much an "achievement" as an attitude. And you can be sure the road to success is paved with ambition and sweat.

Where did this behavior come from? Successful people tend to act instinctively when they see opportunities. What is not often recognized is that they made bad decisions too. How did they recover?

They had a lot of self-confidence to begin with. They didn't lose it when they made bad decisions. They recognized what went wrong, did not agonize over it, and recovered fast. A little pain, in the form of failure, can be a help on the road to success.

Last time you talked with someone you regard as truly successful, did you notice that you were superior in certain ways?

Spirituality

Zen... does not confuse spirituality with thinking about God while one is peeling potatoes.
Zen spirituality is just to peel the potatoes.

—*Alan Watts, philosopher*

The real way to spirituality is "just let it happen." Don't think about it. Intellectualize it. Or otherwise distract yourself. Just focus on what's important and let the rest go.

As I said in the introduction to this book, the very word spirituality used to turn me off. That's because I associated the word with religion, with the emphasis on "organized." Memorize the rule book. Follow the rituals and you will find spirituality. Not likely.

I don't disagree with attempts to systematize spiritual things through religion. How can a man who advises others to "get a system" object when spirituality becomes the subject of organization?

Rituals can be helpful guides. Rules can help steer us in the right direction. The trouble is when rituals and rules become ends in themselves. It's difficult to keep from being trapped. Rituals become fixed rites. Rules become dogma. Our original reason for the systematization becomes lost. When that happens we stop thinking and feeling. We lose touch with spirituality or Gutfeeling. We're in touch only with rituals and rules. Spontaneity is lost.

The thing to remember is that spirituality is the search for meaning in our lives. But how do we find that meaning? Especially in today's environment.

Read the newspaper in the morning. Listen to the news at noon. Watch the evening news on television. A steady diet of this stuff can lead to us being overwhelmed by events. The issues are so hugely abstract and diverse they create a sense of helplessness and insecurity. How can an individual cope with international terrorism, economic collapse, global warming, natural catastrophes, and his or her own personal problems?

Yet the solution is simple. Focus on one problem at a time. Break it down. Change the pieces that are possible to change. Peel the potatoes.

The meaning you are searching for will come as you succeed in these smaller tasks. It has been said that our only real security is our ability to change. We have the ability to change not only ourselves but also circumstances around us. In the power to survive and even to thrive in what seems like hopeless circumstances, you will expand your connection to your own spirituality.

How many times have you caught yourself doing one thing, while thinking simultaneously about three others? Stop. Peel the potatoes.

Synchronicity

When things happen by "accident,"
I always know I am being encouraged to look in that direction.

— George Hancocks, writer

George, my assistant, had a synchronistic experience when we began to write this chapter. He subscribes to the Merriam-Webster "Word of the Day" service on the Internet. He had just begun work on this section, when he thought to get a proper definition. He turned to his trusty dictionary...and the Word of the Day was "synchronicity." The meaning fits the experience perfectly: "The coincidental occurrence of events and especially psychic events that seem related but are not explained by conventional mechanisms of causality."

The concept is linked to the psychology of Carl Jung. He didn't actually coin the word. The "simultaneousness" sense of the word was already in use, according to Merriam-Webster. But Jung gave it special importance in his writings. Meaningful coincidences play an important role in our lives, he believed. Today, some people even look to synchronicities for spiritual guidance.

I believe synchronicity and Gutfeeling are related, and that so-called "coincidences" are meant to call our conscious attention to important factors in our lives. Synchronicities are not really coincidences at all. They may happen because you are intensely concentrated on something and are receptive to anything that reinforces that concentration.

The key aspect here is your "receptiveness." You are open to other suggestions, other influences. You are ready to think in a different way, to open yourself to intuition. In this respect, synchronicities are like a finger pointing the way, emphasizing that you are on the right (or wrong) track.

That is exactly the mode you need to be in to experience Gutfeeling. Be open, be receptive, "Be not afraid!"

When did you last have the feeling
that things happened for a reason?

Teamwork

One man alone can be pretty dumb,
but for real bona-fide stupidity, there ain't nothin'
can beat teamwork.

—Edward Abbey, conservationist

It may not be quite that bad, but no team could ever have created *As You Like It* or the Mona Lisa or the statue of David. Nor would we expect one to. These are all products of a single individual's driving creative genius.

In many human activities, however, progress is impossible without teamwork. Think of police investigation teams, emergency room crews, engineering design groups, television and movie production crews.

Good teamwork depends on Gutfeeling, as any football coach will tell you. In a group, probing questions and open minds often result in a kind of group intuition that could not have emerged without the group environment.

Good teamwork also depends on good leaders. And team success often depends upon how well these leaders lead.

Suffering through dull meetings compares with being on a slow boat to China. Meetings can, however, have great value. They allow for input from many different sources. That can make the results from team effort more effective than results from individual effort. The sum of all the parts is, in fact, not equal to, but greater than, the whole.

That's the theory, and that's what synergy is all about. Successful teamwork involves good leaders and willing team members. The job of leaders is to coax out of group members their best efforts. The job of team members is to suspend their prejudices. Then to submit, from their special expertise, whatever will best contribute to the work. When the job is done, all can say, "We did this ourselves."

Having participated in successful (as well as unsuccessful) groups, I can say from experience that group decisions are more likely to be implemented than individual decisions. The experience itself, with a working group that really swings, can be exciting. That's especially true if there are a lot of individuals in the group who are willing to set aside their egos to achieve something for "the greater good."

*When was the last time
that you participated in a really hard-working, successful group?
What was the secret of its success?*

Time

If you sit on a hot stove, five minutes are forever.
If you have a girl on your lap, five minutes are nothing.

—*Albert Einstein, physicist*

The only non-renewable resource is time. When it's gone, it's gone. Life is not fair, but one thing is sure: Everyone gets only sixty minutes in an hour, twenty-four hours in a day, and no more.

If you learn to listen to your Gutfeeling, you might achieve more. Those who are more successful don't have more time than others. They spend it on more productive activities.

Most of us waste a lot of time doing unimportant things, which makes us feel good. Then, suddenly, we have to do important tasks that might take a long time, yet have to be done instantly. This will create a vicious circle of spending time just to straighten out things that should have been done a long time ago. You run around with a bucket putting out fires. However, if you spend more of your time on important tasks, you can avoid that trap.

Certain things in life can't be changed. Nature takes time. If a woman gets pregnant, it takes her nine months to give birth. If nine women are impregnated at once, you still won't get one baby in one month. You'll get nine babies in nine months.

Remember, your Gutfeeling does not always give you the right answer, especially on time management. But it's a reliable benchmark.

Sometimes it seems to me that time is not only relative, it is also subjective and elastic. It stretches endlessly before you when you're young, but passes faster when you're older. The more you hate to do a job, the slower the time will pass. The more you enjoy the task, the faster the time will fly.

The poet T.S. Eliot recognized that time is "fluid" when he wrote these lines in his book *Four Quartets*:

Time present and time past
Are both perhaps present in time future,
And time future contained in time past.
If all time is eternally present
All time is unredeemable.

Remember, be gracious with people and ruthless with your time!

You have just read 360 words. You probably spent two minutes reading and understanding this section. If you're a slow reader, like me, it took you 3.5 minutes. But we both read it. Regard the time spent as an investment and ask yourself how it will improve you.

If you listen to your Gutfeeling,
how will you spend the next ten minutes?

Trust

*Trust your gut feeling
more than your logic.*

— Popular saying

Trusting means you are placing your confidence in somebody. You are making judgements about their character, abilities, strengths, and respect for the truth. Most of the time those judgements sound logical but are based on emotion.

There is an old saying that it's better to trust one who is frequently in error than one who is never in doubt. But why would you place your confidence in someone who makes mistakes? Because making mistakes, if the individual learns from them, shows responsibility and maturity. If you are going to do this, you want to make sure the person who receives it is capable of growth. Growth is an ongoing process for everybody.

Trust is one of those intangibles. It's a Gutfeeling in a class by itself.

It's easier to describe what it isn't than what it is. When someone says, "I don't trust that person," you know immediately what is meant. But in fact, you don't *know*. You "feel" what is meant. You feel the person is "suspect," not reliable, perhaps even deceitful. The untrusted person could have many more "bad" characteristics.

Thinking about trust is a good way to get a handle on Gutfeeling itself. Think about the people *you* trust. Think about what that means to you. Are you dealing with the hard facts? With reason?

You may be. You may have facts and knowledge of that person's past life which lead you to believe he or she is "trustworthy." You may even be able to analyze those facts and come to a rational conclusion.

But you are far more likely to have a "sense" of whether that person is trustworthy or not. Your emotion and Gutfeeling play a big role in trust. You have done the analysis, laid out the facts. You must still take that leap of faith.

You must trust or suspend judgement. If you suspend judgement, you do not trust. Trust is a feeling, an emotion, an intuition. It may be based on facts, but it is one of those rare Gutfeelings that will not let you off the hook. You must acknowledge it, therefore "trust"—or not.

What are the steps you take in trusting others?

Underpaid & overworked

There are two things people want more than sex and money:
Recognition and praise.

—Mary Kay Ash, business executive

Recognition and praise drive all of us. Mary Kay Ash's description fits 99.99% of the population. Ask individual workers. They see themselves as underpaid, overworked, and undervalued. But if you probe a little you will quickly find they're not too upset about the work and the money. They are starving for recognition and praise!

If you ask their bosses, they most likely say that their employees are overpaid, underworked, and overvalued. Who is right? Maybe neither. Bosses could immediately become leaders if they recognized the need for personal recognition and praise. Don't be quite so stinting with kind words. What might it cost, apart from some unnecessary pride?

You can talk negatively about your own car. You might even refer to it as an old rustbucket, a lemon, or a piece of junk. But if I ask you, "Did you come to work in your old piece of junk today?" you'll probably get very upset with me. It's okay for you to belittle something of your own (maybe even tongue-in-cheek), but I don't have the same privilege. You would regard it as a bad case of "bad-mouthing" and would resent it.

The same holds true for your spouse. You might call your better half "the sloppy, stupid old ____." One of my friends used to refer to his mother (affectionately) as "the old bag." I've heard husbands referred to as "old beer-guts" or "the couch potato." But let someone else refer to him or her in those terms, and watch out!

If you make the right decision, using your Gutfeeling, you will call it one of your skills.

If you make the wrong decision, you will blame it on Gutfeeling.

When did you last think you were underpaid, overworked, and undervalued?

Value

One does not get paid for the hour,
but for the value one brings to the hour.
— Peter Urs Bender

Value is a perception of worth, and Aristotle had it right. Our perceptions of worth depend upon our awareness. Are we awake to the relativity of value?

Even in business we use terms like book value, breakup value, and actual cash value. In mathematics we use terms like absolute value, characteristic value, expected value, and critical value. All values are relative. To what? To our perceptions.

There are material and spiritual values. There are values that add to each and values that add to all. They apply to goods and services, to numerical quantities, to the relative lengths of musical tones, or to the lightness and darkness of color.

If you perceive spirituality, Gutfeeling, and instinct as of low value, you are likely to pay little attention to them. If, however, you perceive they have high value, as many outstanding business people do, you will likely pursue them. Use them as positive guides in your life.

All too often, however, "value" is equated with "cost"—what you are prepared to "pay" for a thing. This is really about monetary value, reduced to its crudest form.

Faced with this paradox, some of our most profound thinkers rate the value of spirituality as "infinite" and its cost as "everything." They see that you really can't place a value on spirituality, so its "cost" becomes infinite too.

Perhaps most of us would not be prepared to go that far, or even want to pursue spirituality to the exclusion of everything else. There is no doubt that value, when considering spirituality, carries with it overtones of a value exceeding its perceived cost.

Have you carefully examined the value you place on spirituality? Give it a second look.

Verhexed

Negative spirituality at work.

— Swiss saying

Sometimes German words need no explanation. So many of them have become standard in our language we use them without thinking. *Verhexed* is one such word. Just the sound of it says "something's not right."

It means "jinxed" or "bewitched." I use it to mean negative spirituality. You may start with good intentions, but somehow, somewhere, everything goes wrong.

Isn't negative spirituality a contradiction in terms? I think not. Imagine the negative spiritual impacts of such emotions as jealousy, envy, and revenge. For every positive emotion, there is a negative one. Trust/suspicion. Love/hate. Are these Gutfeelings? Yes. They're the other side of the coin. Sometimes we just let our worst instincts take over.

There is no easy route to cease being *verhexed*. But first one must recognize what's happening. Then one must substitute a positive emotion or feeling for the negative one.

You have to work at it, but it can be done. Remember that a negative Gutfeeling will eat away at you and reduce your overall energy. Maintaining it is a lot harder than replacing it.

Remember the old law of motion? It's easier to keep a thing in motion than to set it in motion.

Next time three things go wrong in three hours,
don't think you're verhexed.
You're just having a bad morning.

Water cooler

*I know a lot of people who could use a few drinks
from the Fountain of Wisdom.*

— Peter Urs Bender

In many companies you often learn what's happening round the water cooler. Rumors are the vehicle.

Learning about spirituality can happen in a similar manner. Many people tend to gather round the water cooler of cultism. They think to pick up the "latest" on spirituality. And there are so many groups that think they have insights into spirituality!

There is a similarity to discovering your spirituality through Water-Cooler Wisdom. Remain sceptical. No need to shut off the information flow. But consider it carefully. Rumor is human. And gossip can be good for you—sometimes.

But gossip creates a lot of anxiety about things that are illusions. It will drain your energy, making you feel depressed. Most of the time, rumors and gossip are negative! Run from them!

*Where is your metaphorical water-cooler located,
and how are you going to turn its gossip into wisdom?*

Well

A source from which something can be drawn as needed.

— Merriam-Webster Online Dictionary

We live in a world where everything is becoming polluted. Fresh water is becoming more and more important. Of course, we all know water is not really "fresh." It's all recycled through nature. Even when it falls from heaven it's polluted with dust particles and other elements.

We never know how many wells are on our property until we search. There was a farmer who inherited a thousand acres of dry land. It was totally useless. It was so dry even cactus didn't have a chance to survive.

Then one day his wife decided to see if anything lay beneath the dry soil. She hired a drilling rig. After three days of drilling—nothing. "Keep going," she demanded. Three more days passed with no result. She insisted on drilling three more days. The crew laughed, but said, "It's your buck, lady." On the ninth day water gushed from the hole, and it was her turn to laugh. She had discovered the property sat atop an aquifer.

Real fresh water comes from a well. Dig for one before you are thirsty. It always pays off. There are no shortcuts to hard work. The elevators are out of work. You have to climb step by step.

Deep inside we all have a well. It holds happiness, joy, rejuvenation. Certain individuals access this well easier than others. They've learned how to locate their spiritual resources.

Let your Gutfeeling tell you where your well is. Use your mental dowsing rod to tell you when and where to look.

When did you last enjoy a thought
that sprang from your own mental well?

Writing

We write to taste life twice, in the moment and in retrospection.

—Anaïs Nin, writer

Writing for yourself is like speaking to yourself. It offers the chance to listen to our own thoughts. We then have the opportunity to clarify them in the privacy of our own minds. It's an adventure, an exploration. Cultivating our own ideas helps us clarify our thoughts, feelings, and actions. But no good letter, brochure, or book was ever created in one sitting. It takes rewrite, rewrite.

With Gutfeeling, it's similar. When one gets a feeling, one has to hold on to it somehow. The idea is to capture it on the fly. Maybe you just want to discuss it with someone else. Having done that, you might want to return to it and give it some more thought.

If your feeling is an intense one, it won't go away. You don't need to worry about it. It will stick with you till you can deal with it. But it's the little ones that can provide valuable clues to self-development. Keep track of them. They can result in personal revelations of great value.

Keeping a logbook is not a bad idea. But don't try to produce a work of art. Your log should just be that, a quick notation of ideas and feelings that occur to you. It's a very personal thing.

That's really how this book began. As I was working on a number of projects at the same time, random thoughts would occur to me. Sometimes they were ideas for speeches or books. Sometimes they were on topics I felt I should explore but couldn't fit into my schedule of priorities.

I didn't labor over getting the idea down in flawlessly correct literary style. I just jotted down words in my marvelous microcomputer log (lots of them even misspelled!). When I felt I had time to consider the creation of another book, lo and behold! I had a virtually ready-made outline. That outline, in turn, helped to organize my thoughts. I had a road map, a set of directions, and a tentative destination.

Many of the fragmentary and fleeting thoughts I recorded have turned into section headings for this book. They were all recorded in single-word form throughout my log—not one after the other, as they were in my finished outline, but one here, one there, one somewhere else. Pulling them together in an outline clarified the direction of my thinking. I knew I had something to say about spirituality and Gutfeeling!

Do you have a logbook file in your computer?
Open one. Try it.
You'll be astonished at the results.

Yellow Pages

The Yellow Pages is now a standard resource. The words have worked their way into our everyday vocabulary. Everyone knows it refers to a directory whose pages are yellow-colored. It's a listing of services, businesses, and governments that do not lend themselves easily to classification in the regular telephone directory. I refer to it as my personal "Fish Pond." Remember that game from when you were a kid?

If ever a book was analytical in nature, the Yellow Pages is. Yet it lends itself to intuitive use. It has become an essential tool for virtually everyone—and now it's online! If you are hunting for basic information on most topics, no matter how exotic, the Yellow Pages is one of the first tools you turn to. If the information you find is not conclusive, at least you know it might point you to something else. And on the Internet there are often electronic links to other sources which may prove to be exactly what you're looking for.

If only we had a directory for Gutfeeling! Unfortunately, it's more elusive than the Yellow Pages. Yet the principle of "searching and finding" is the same. You must always start with a question.

When I looked in my Yellow Pages I even found a listing for Religious Organizations between the listings for Religious Goods and Relocation Services. They are listed by alphabet, not by religion, so they're all mixed up together. There were phone numbers of Christian groups, and for many other religions. Buddhists, Moslems, Hindus, Mormons, and Eastern Orthodox churches.

Those references would have led me to other information, had I wished to pursue them. In fact it's a good idea to check out your own business or industry on the Internet to remind yourself of the breadth and depth of the field in which you work.

It's the same with Gutfeeling. You start with a question. Where is it? If you're serious, you have to reply to yourself.

Emeril Lagasse, the showman chef of FoodTV, breaks his audiences up when he shouts, "I said to myself, 'Self! Where do I go from here?'" But you can tell he's serious. He really does pose questions to himself. And he expects Self to answer, no matter how crazy the response.

If you're not sure where to start, phrase your questions as bluntly as Emeril. When do you feel Gutfeeling? (Wait for the answer.) Does it come as a subtle hint, or as a strong intuition to follow a specific path? (Wait for it.) If the answer seems inconclusive, don't worry. Try again.

Make listening to yourself a habit. Make a game of it. Pick the name mode you want and ask away. Ask yourself questions about Gutfeeling regularly. You may not have the Yellow Pages in your mind, but you'll quickly get answers you might not have expected.

Self! Talk to me when I ask you a question.
What do I feel in my gut about this?

Youth

It is not possible for civilization to flow backwards while there is youth in the world. Youth may be headstrong but it will advance its allotted length.

—Helen Keller, educator

Sometimes I think youth doesn't have a clue when it comes to Gutfeeling. Other times I wish I had its intuitive grasp of the fundamentals.

Remembering my own youth, I can say that once I became a conscious person, I quickly sensed when things were going in the right direction—or not. I never realized this was Gutfeeling until I became an adult and was able to analyze those feelings.

As a child being unable to explain these feelings didn't mean I didn't feel them. We often say that youth acts on impulse. I think youth acts intuitively, often instantly. Youth doesn't stop to analyze feelings, then carefully plot a course of action. Youth feels. Youth acts. There is no conscious analysis.

This is a Zen-like state of being, and one of the reasons why Zen teachers refer to the Zen state as becoming a child again. Not *like* becoming, but *becoming* a child again. Many philosophers, the Zen masters, and even Jesus recognized the intuitive nature of child life. They all recommended adults follow the same path.

It's not a "simple" pattern of life for an adult. It's very complex. But it's complex only because as we grow up most of us are trained not to listen to our intuition or "impulsive" feelings. That's a pity, because those impulses are tied directly to our Gutfeeling.

Even to get back in touch with our child self requires an act of letting go. It means you should say to yourself, from time to time, "What did I feel about this as a kid?" If you can begin to get answers to questions like these, you are slowly getting in touch with your essential inner feelings. Let it happen.

Do you allow your inner child to come out of you once in a while?

Venture Capital

Nothing ventured, nothing gained.

— Anon.

Risk. That's the word most associated with Venture Capital. In fact, risk is a major aspect of life. No pain, no gain, is one way of expressing it.

But risk doesn't mean rushing into the first venture that occurs to you. Careful risk-taking is always preceded by careful analysis.

And that's the way you should approach any decision-making in your own life. I have always liked the "make-a-list" approach. Put down the pros and cons on a single page. Compare and contrast them. Sometimes the logic of the analysis says "Stop!" almost before you get started. If that's what your analysis indicates, forget about it. Don't go forward. You'll be sorry if you do. However, remember we regret more things we have not done than things we did wrong. And it doesn't take much Gutfeeling to assess the risk if all the pointers are negative. It is also better to learn to apologize than to ask for permission.

But often there is a balance. If this, then that. What is best? That's where you need to think about it carefully. Do your analysis, then sleep on it. Don't rush into anything, but don't be afraid to take a bold step if your Gutfeeling says you can make a go of it.

Venture capitalists seek greater rewards for taking an investment risk. So should you. If you have done your homework you should be able to predict what your return might be down the line, and whether or not the payoff is worth the risk. I'm not just talking in monetary reward terms here, but in terms of emotional enrichment.

When did you last scare your pants off?

Zero-based budgeting

On the starting line, we all feel the energy.

— Peter Urs Bender

You might have been a kid or in your teens. But once-upon-a-time you were on a starting line. You waited for the signal...then you were off!

Zero-based budgeting is a wonderful term and concept. It's the process of starting each fiscal year with a budget of zero. There are no holdovers from last year. No slush funds. No surpluses. You start each year with a clean slate and go from there. It forces business to review the whole operation. Constantly looking for savings and efficiencies.

It's a concept that should be applied to our personal lives. A zero-based budget would see us start every year with a clean slate. It should include a series of believable and attainable goals, not an impossible list of dreams.

At least one of those goals should be to watch and listen for your Gutfeeling. I am also a firm believer that it pays to renew this goal from time to time.

Take the zero-based budgeting route. Review, renew, and revise your "budget" at regular intervals. If once a year seems too long, make the review period shorter. But do it. It's a wonderful feeling to start from scratch. Put the old period behind you. Plan the new period afresh. Don't carry old failures—Atlas carrying the world on his shoulders. Let them go. Then resolve to plan again.

Think of sunset laws. They force legislators to clear the statute books of old and outdated legislation—or rewrite it for the times. Do the same.

Think of the energy you have on a new job you've taken on. Can you remember what it was like?

Zen

The rules are there are no rules.
The system is there is no system.

— Zen in a nutshell

Almost everyone in the Western world today is familiar with the Japanese concept of Zen. Quite a few even understand what Zen is all about. At least they think they do.

Zen, like Gutfeeling, is indefinable. Those who describe it as a "system" of belief should stop right there. Zen, like Gutfeeling, just *is*. If there is anything Zen isn't, it's a "system." It's about as anti-system a system as humans are capable of having!

In fact, even trying to describe it in system terms is misleading, as the Zen sages themselves insist. Zen is not about "having," or "possessing," or "following the rules." It's about "letting go," "being," "doing," and "feeling."

It's "the unbearable lightness of being" in one unforgettable phrase. Or as one Zen master said of his own enlightenment: "It's the same as before, only three feet above the ground."

To us, these phrases and descriptions may not make much sense. That's because they're trying to define the indefinable. The only way to do that is with metaphor. Zen devotees themselves often refuse to describe their states of mind. That's why Zen teachers often use gestures and "riddles" to try to jolt students out of their customary learned patterns of thought. And that's what I'm trying to do with this book, too. Jolt your consciousness into awareness.

This can make Zen maddening to Westerners who are programmed to "understand" everything they can. The act of understanding relies on definition and analysis, the very opposite of Zen.

Yet opposites are not always destructive, and the Zen approach should not seem so mysterious to us. In the Christian religion there is a saying: "The service of the Lord is perfect freedom." It seems like a contradiction in terms, but it's not. I don't mean that "serving the Lord" is the only way to go. It could simply mean releasing yourself into your profession, your job, your hobby, your family. The phrase is simply a way of saying that letting go of "self" in any action releases the mental energy leashed within us. Thus, we become free of the "system" while still remaining part of it.

The rules are there are no rules.
The system is there is no system.

Most of us get flashes of intuition from time to time. We have "hunches" that a situation or life is going this way or that way. If you "let go" of conscious control, your intuition or Gutfeeling will talk to you. When you are required to make a decision, you'll make it with your whole mind, instead of just the conscious part of it.

To "hear the sound of one hand clapping" should be your goal in everything you do. What is that sound? It is no sound. That's the answer to the riddle, but "an answer" is not the goal. The goal is to experience the sound of one hand clapping in everything you do.

When did you last pause, focusing your consciousness, to meditate?

The Final Word

The Final Word is never the Last Word!

What I have to say about Gutfeeling is coming to an end. But the Last Words, the Best Words, are yours.

What I hope you found in this book is a sense of where to look for your Gutfeeling. In telling you to seek it, I am not asking you to search for something that isn't there. I am not trying to identify a "right" or "wrong" path, or to suggest there is only one way to go.

Listen. You will hear it. It won't be someone who calls you and leaves you a message on your voicemail. However, it may be. Nothing is impossible. We have to learn to listen to Gutfeeling. Often we just override it. But there is an inner voice.

Watch. The chances you'll see it on TV are very slim. But you might see it in your dreams. You might even see it in your mind during a busy meeting. Or when driving a car. But you have to look for it.

Believe. You have to believe you will experience it. Give it time and understanding and you will experience it.

This book was never designed to make miracles. But if it does, I am happy for you. Nor is it a quick-fix remedy. If you're interested in quick fixes, you should never read any of my books. None of them say that the steps I recommend are easy. And yet they are not *complicated*. All you have to do is work away at it. Day by day.

Big buildings are built piece by piece. The largest freestanding structure in the world was built stage by stage. That's the way I would suggest you tackle finding your Gutfeeling. Work at it a little every day. John Robert Colombo, my text editor, recommends that you "Do one weird thing a week."

Some people do things that are unpredictable. Why is one more successful than another? Often it's not because they have a better education or other advantages. It's because they see opportunities where others see stumbling blocks.

How do they see them? I believe it was because of their intuition. Their ability to listen, watch, and believe in their Gutfeeling. They are able to listen and follow feelings that are basically indescribable and unexplainable.

Look at **Mahatma Gandhi**. His biographers pay tribute to intuition as one of the key elements in his campaign to gain independence for India. "Gandhi's protests, spontaneous, unpredictable, and guided by intuition, confounded the British, as did the protestors' courage in the face of superior arms," says one biography.

Yet Gandhi was not born spiritual and saintly. He worked hard to gain it. He changed himself and his actions time and again in the face of scholastic failure and an unhappy marriage. At the beginning he could not even make a living as a lawyer. For instance, in his first case before the bar, he was so inept he was unable to open his mouth. Yet this great social and religious leader, when tried for sedition by the British, turned his own trial into an eloquent condemnation of imperialism.

This seeming early failure became one of the Twentieth Century's icons, and in the words of the social thinker and writer Lewis Mumford he was "the most important religious figure of our time." When Gandhi was once asked his secret, he responded simply, "Renounce and enjoy."

Ray Kroc, founder of the McDonald's Restaurant chain, must have had several key Gutfeeling moments in his life, the first of which led directly to the second. In both cases he saw possibilities where others saw nothing.

Born in 1902 in Oak Park, Illinois, Kroc worked at various jobs until 1937, when he met the inventor of an ingenious, five-spindle beater called the "Multimixer." He saw its possibilities in the restaurant business immediately. He invested his life savings to purchase exclusive marketing rights. From then until 1954, he enthusiastically sold the machines to the trade.

In that same year he learned of a restaurant in California that had purchased eight of the mixers for their burger-and-shakes operation. The name of the restaurant was McDonald's. Inspired by what he saw when he visited the operation, he also saw the franchise opportunity and struck a deal with the McDonald brothers. The rest is history.

He bought the McDonald brothers out for $2.7 million in 1961. At the time of his death in 1984, the McDonald's chain had more than 7,500 outlets internationally, and annual sales of $8 billion. Kroc's pioneering methods in the fast food industry have been compared to Henry Ford's revolutionary contribution to the automobile industry.

Kroc also established a generous policy of charitable giving for the chain. The life of his company even touched that of Gandhi's. His wife, after his death, contributed $25 million to the University of San Diego to establish the Mohandas K. Gandhi Institute for Peace and Justice.

Walt Disney is forever immortalized in Mickey Mouse. His fantasies from his own childhood have created some of the most heart-warming movies of all time. They have also been translated into theme parks for adults and children worldwide.

A shrewd businessman, Disney nevertheless relied on his instincts when it came to making final decisions. A good example is the question put to him by a reporter about the movie *Fantasia*. "When *Fantasia* was not well received by the public, what did you do then?" he was asked.

"I put '*Dumbo*' together and I just started with a little idea. And I just kept expanding it. First, I was going to make it as about a thirty-minute subject. But as I got developing and we got little new things in there, I kept expanding and before I knew it, I had a sixty-two minute picture that cost $700,000. And when it reached that point I said, 'That's as far as I can stretch it.' They said, 'Can't you add another ten minutes to it, Walt?' And I said, 'No. That other ten minutes is liable to cost another half million dollars.' You can stretch a thing so far and then it just won't hold. So I said, 'No. That's the length.'"

By the time of his death in 1966, the Disney studio's output amounted to 21 full-length animated films, 493 short subjects, 47 live-action films, seven True-Life Adventure features, 330 hours of Mickey Mouse Club television programs, 78 half-hour *Zorro* television adventures, and 280 other television shows. In virtually every project, Disney's intuition about them shone through.

In this book, all I want to do is help you to find your own Gutfeeling. I want you to gain more confidence about it, and to listen to it. Will it always help you work things out for the better? No, it won't. Gandhi faced some awful failures. Disney went bankrupt early in his career. Kroc fought a lifelong battle with diabetes.

Remember that in life every bad thing has some good in it. Take forest fires, for instance. When they occur they are massive environmental events whose consequences seem horrifying and drastic. But fire is nature's cleanser. It cleans out old forest growth and creates an opportunity for the forest to renew itself.

Remember that in life every good thing has some bad in it.

Think about the people who win lotteries. Sudden and unaccustomed wealth can often lead to great unhappiness and difficulty. I have nothing against lotteries or lottery-winners. I just hope, whenever I see a winner announced, that he or she has the ability to cope with such sudden good fortune.

Can we see these changes?

The best is to find out by yourself where you feel the positive intuitions. Where do you feel them? Heart, toes, fingers...? We're not the experts. You are. You tell us.

If you found the voice and you listen to it, it could help you to make more right decisions. However, I want to make it perfectly clear that if you're playing roulette and your Gutfeeling says, "Put it all on black," and you lose, it's not my fault.

Where do we go from here? Learn to listen and learn to feel and learn to trust your Gutfeeling. Everybody is different. It might take longer, it might not. Expand your horizons!

A wise man can learn from a fool.
A fool never learns.

F~AQ~

*A fool may answer more questions in an hour
than a wise man can answer in seven years.*

— English proverb

Will Gutfeeling help my sex life?

It certainly should. In love and sex, intuition plays a much greater role than logic and analysis. How many times have you heard someone complaining that so-and-so is "not romantic"? For "romantic" substitute the word "intuitive." When you're in love, let yourself go. You'll discover how much Gutfeeling can do for you! (*See also* Love.)

Do I have to work at Gutfeeling, or will it come on its own?

Yes, and no—and here's why. Gutfeeling, especially if you are not used to recognizing it, can be elusive. You have to learn to identify it before you can catch it. But the worst way to go about it is to say to yourself, "I can't feel Gutfeeling. I should be able to. Why can't I? Worry, worry worry...." All you're doing at that point is creating stress for yourself, with no results. (*See also* Growth.)

Your first objective should be to identify a single Gutfeeling in yourself. Then, hopefully, more than one. Once you can recognize these intuitions, you will come to recognize what triggers them in you. That's when you start to use them more systematically. Then you can work at bringing them out and acting on them. The more of them you have, the easier they will emerge. Allow them to come out and depend on them as part of your thinking/feeling process. We are saying: "Let go, and they'll come to you." (*See also* Habits.)

This is not a contradiction in terms. Think of athletes. They have to work hard to learn the skills they perform. Once they reach a certain level, however, they have to "relax into" the activities they are performing. It's the same with Gutfeeling. (*See also* Golf.)

The working at it part is when you apply your analytical faculties to Gutfeeling. You can't analyze the feeling itself, but you can set it in a rational field. Ask yourself a question like "If I don't follow my instinct, what will be the result?" Then list all the pro's and con's. Balance your list. Make your decision. You will gain the benefit of both instinct and analysis.

Can I believe in organized religion and not be spiritual?
Yes. Being a member of any organized religion does not guarantee spirituality. But spirituality is part of organized religion. In fact, without it, that religion would die out. A religion without spirituality is like a rose without thorns. Possible, but unlikely. What happens often, however, is that the rituals involved in organized religion strangle spirituality. True spirituality cannot be channeled in any "approved" manner. It has to come from within. (*See also* Religion.)

Can I be spiritual without belonging to organized religion?
Yes again. Organized religion has no monopoly on spirituality. In fact, as stated at the beginning of this book, "Spirituality does not come from religion. Religion comes from spirituali-

ty." (*See also* Introduction.) Therefore, you can enjoy spirituality with or without religion.

Do women have more Gutfeeling than men?

Not more, but they are more likely to listen to it more often. Men are often raised to be macho, stiff-upper-lip, don't-cry individuals. This behavior training inhibits emotions and encourages men to ignore their feelings. Women are more often raised to pay attention to their feelings, and hence are more in tune with their emotions. It's not a hard-and-fast rule, but it's felt that women are "more intuitive" than men. This simply means they're more used to adding emotional content to their decisions than basing them, as men are supposed to do, on reason and logic alone. (*See also* For Men Only.)

How does Gutfeeling differ from intuition or instinct?

Gutfeeling, intuition, and hunch are much the same thing. Instinct, however, is inbred. Your body does certain things whether you think about them or not. Your heart beats, you breathe, your blood circulates. You must remember to eat, but once having eaten your body does the rest without any intervention from you. Yet there is also a sense in which instinct is part of Gutfeeling. You can stop yourself from doing certain things we call instinctual so there is a Gutfeeling component to instinct as well. Think of the fight-or-flight response. It's automatic. But we can control it. When to control it is the question. Your Gutfeeling will give you hints. (*See also* Instinct.)

I have never had a Gutfeeling. How will I recognize one?

You probably have had a Gutfeeling, but have not recognized it as such. The thing to do is to watch for the tell-tale signs outlined below. And remember. There are none so deaf as those who will not hear.

Is Gutfeeling culture?
Not really, if what you mean by culture is environment. But if you mean by culture that pattern of knowledge, belief, and behavior that makes us human, including our beliefs, attitudes, goals, and practices—then yes, Gutfeeling is a part of our culture.

What happens when Gutfeeling takes me over?
Gutfeeling really doesn't "take you over." It's a feeling, an intuition, a "tingling in your fingertips," what Albert Einstein called *"Fingerspitzengefühl."* Or a sudden sense that "there's more behind this than meets the eye." When you experience it, listen. Your subconscious is trying to tell you something. Have you ever experienced someone telling you something that you feel is slightly off-color, that it is not right, and it makes you feel uncomfortable? That's Gutfeeling. Your job now is to mark it, remember it, and come back to it when you're alone and can examine the feeling. It will tell you a lot about how to go on. (*See also* Gutfeeling.)

Why is Gutfeeling capitalized and spelled as one word?
Gutfeeling is an unintentional play on words. George and I were looking for a title for the book. We did not want to call it simply "Spirituality at Work." George suggested Gut Feelings. When I wrote it down I wrote it as one word— "Gutfeeling." George immediately recognized that the English word "Gut," which is another name for "intuition," is the same as the German word "Gut," which means "good." A combination of Good and Gut produces Good Feelings, and that's how it came about.

Will Gutfeeling replace logic?
Never. In fact, too much Gutfeeling can mislead you. Use logic, analysis, and intuition together. Do your rational analy-

sis. Make sure it holds together, as you would with any business plan or proposal. Then wait. Sleep on it. Try to get a "feel" for the way you think about it. That's where your Gutfeeling can tell you whether to "hold or fold." (*See also* Accounting.)

How can I learn to utilize Gutfeeling?
Remember the old words you learned at school about paying attention to traffic? Stop. Look. Listen. Then act. It's that simple and that complex.

Interesting sites on the web

Not everything that is on the web is real—
not everything that is real is on the web.

—Peter Urs Bender

Websites go on and off the web every day. But the sites we have chosen for you here are very stable. None of the sites are religious in nature, as of now.

They are all about self-development. They have been around for quite a while on the same web address, although many are changing all the time. When a website address changes, there is usually some notice as well. If it's a site you refer to you'll be able to bookmark the new site and your use of it will continue uninterrupted. If your interests are in self-development, you'll find something on every one of these sites to help you. Good luck!

www.AddEQ.com
This is Dr. Michael E. Rock's site. It will give you more background and insight into Emotional Quotient (EQ) than any of the other sites. But plan to spend some time on it. It's not a site you can absorb in a few minutes.

www.AddEQCommunity.com
More of an Emotional Quotient community site from Dr. Michael Rock. Very useful if you are planning to utilize EQ in training. Its self-described mission "is to link the diverse EQ needs of individuals and organizations with resources and capabilities in the world using the extraordinary reach of the internet."

www.Adm.UWaterloo.ca
For a real workout, try this site. You'll come away with a good feeling for your own spiritual values, as well as some hard advice on how to proceed and where you might go given your value set. It will take more than a few minutes of your time. The full address is: www.adm.uwaterloo.ca.infocecs/CRC/manual/values.html

www.BeMoreCreative.com
Entering this site is like finding the mother lode of creative quotations and stimulating ideas. Its webmaster, Frank Baer, has put together a remarkable database, to which this author owes a debt of gratitude. The sub-address is /home.cq.htm.

www.Biography.com
If you're looking for other examples of outstanding personalities who must have listened to their Gutfeeling, this is the place to go. Enter the name of the person you're interested in, and up pops the biography.

www.DavidEck.com
Offers a great variety of interesting tests, such as personality, IQ, love, health, career, fun. This takes a less academic approach to the subject of testing. You can have a lot of fun here.

http:/DiscoveryHealth.Queendom.com
There are more than 30 tests listed on this site, which describes itself as "serious entertainment." It offers another opportunity to get a handle on many aspects of your character. One is Emotional Intelligence. It involves 70 questions and it takes 35-40 minutes to complete. The site is part of the discoveryhealth.com website.

www.Disney.com

The Walt Disney Family Museum is a fascinating compendium of items from Walt's early life, and contains a first-rate biography of the man himself.

www.EiConsortium.org

There is a mass of information on this site about Emotional Intelligence. Lots of information to download. Well worth spending some time on.

www.Heartskills.com

A very interesting site that helps you come to grips with your Emotional Quotient, or Emotional Intelligence. Worth exploring if you ask yourself the question, "Have I ever experienced Gutfeeling?" and the answer is "No." A good site to broaden your knowledge anyway.

www.IChing.com

The great *Book of Changes* is now available on a website. If you use this site or the book as it is meant to be used—as a guide to explore your subconscious thoughts—you will find it fascinating. Remember, it doesn't tell fortunes, but it can help you to sort out your mental priorities.

www.PeterUrsBender.com

This website includes a great deal of background about Peter as a speaker and author, as well as a neat Personality Analysis Quiz that will take you only a few minutes to complete. It will give you an insight into your own character.

www.2h.com

If you like taking EQ and IQ tests, the ultimate site is this one. Test it to your heart's content. You may even learn something! This site might be described as "IQ tests as a form of Gaming." Still, it's fascinating.

The Feedback Page

*Make sure you have someone in your life
from whom you can get reflective feedback.*

— Warren Bennis, business author

Everything comes and goes. Things get better or worse. Nothing stays the same. This book won't either, especially if you would like to contribute to it.

I thought I'd ask you, my readers, for your personal feedback. My objective is to make this book as useful as possible. Have a look at the questions below. Would you like to be part of another edition? Answer them and get back to me.

Did this book help you? In what way? How could I make this book better? Do you have a personal story to share about Gutfeeling?

If you want to send me your thoughts, feelings, and experiences, I would feel honored. I might make use of them in a future edition. Of course, I will check back with you before anything appears in print, so be sure to send me both your regular address and your email address. Send your feedback to:

Gutfeeling@PeterUrsBender.com

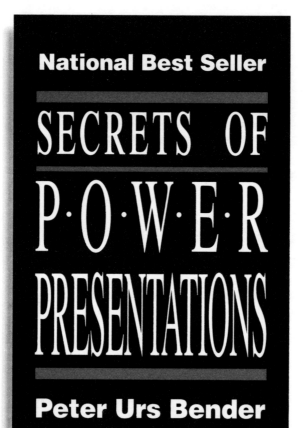

Stepping away from the lectern and speaking without notes was the best idea for me.
WALTER SCHMID,
Zurich, Switzerland

Using more powerful body language, voice and visuals to reinforce the message really helped me.
DONNA EARL,
San Francisco, USA

I especially like the tips on how to effectively open and close my presentation.
GERRY KENDALL,
Tel Aviv, Israel

National Best Seller

SECRETS OF

P·O·W·E·R

PRESENTATIONS

Peter Urs Bender

Thanks to Power Presentations I wowed my clients at my last sales presentation.
ROBERT PALZER,
Nelson, New Zealand

Money is power. Presenting with power is everything.
DR. JERRY WHITE,
Toronto, Canada

Easy to read–simple to follow. Very helpful.
LESLIE BAGSHAW,
Chicago, USA

Secrets of Power Presentations

There are hundreds of books on Presentations. The reason *Secrets of Power Presentations* is different is because it contains the main points covered in most of them. But this book organizes them in a simple and easy-to-understand way, into five elements. Here are a few insights from this book.

THE SPEECH
Has to inform, entertain, and move to action.

BODY LANGUAGE
Dress Powerful
Stand Powerful
Think and Feel Powerful

EQUIPMENT
Warning: mechanical devices can sense when you're in a hurry!

ENVIRONMENT
To change one's thinking pattern, change the environment.

PREPARATION
Perfect Prior Preparation Prevents Poor Performance!

If two equally educated and qualified people offer similar solutions to a problem –the one who knows how to present with power will always have a much better chance of having his/her ideas implemented.

Powerful, impressive and lasting presentations start from within…

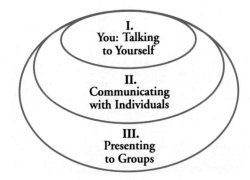

Secrets of Power Presentations is not a quick fix. It's a reference. It does not need to be read from beginning to end, but a smart presenter will read it through. Use it as a reference manual. Each chapter, part and subtitle is designed as a stand-alone module.

www.PeterUrsBender.com

SECRETS TO DELIVERING A POWERFUL SPEECH

- Fit your topic to your audience's interests. Communicate in their language.
- Organize your presentation. Know your main points well.
- Never read your speech from a text. Use minimal notes.
- Practice and rehearse your speech over and over. Preferably in front of real people. Otherwise on your feet.
- Dramatize, emphasize, energize.
- Pause frequently.
- Tell them you are looking forward to your presentation.
- Start slowly and then gradually speed up to a comfortable pace. Look happy and confident. Smile.

SECRETS TO IMPROVE YOUR BODY LANGUAGE

- Love your body. If you are a bit overweight, adore your figure anyway.
- Stand and sit to your tallest. Never slouch.
- Always wear your best clothes.
- Move slowly, deliberately, and gracefully.
- Never rush in front of your audience. Shoulders back. Chest out. Chin up. Smile!

SECRETS ON EFFECTIVE USE OF EQUIPMENT

- Confirm twice that all your equipment will be available on time at your location.
- Check and re-check light bulbs, electrical power, cable connections, outlets and contacts, switches and any moving parts.
- Prepare your notes on your flip charts and overhead transparencies at least three days before you present.
- Arrange to have back-up equipment close by and be prepared to present without visuals. Carry your overhead transparencies, slides, and handouts (at least one set) yourself to ensure they will not be lost.

Secrets to Creating An Effective Environment

- Arrive at your presentation room the day before or at least one hour prior to your talk.
- Turn on the air conditioning or open all the windows to allow fresh air into the room.
- Know where all the light switches are hidden. Find out the purpose of all other switches on the walls so you do not touch the wrong ones.
- Put out fewer chairs than you know will be used. Stack the rest at the back of the room.
- Put a "Reserved" sign in the last row of chairs to encourage people to sit close to the front.
- Close the curtains.
- Locate all telephones in your presentation room and arrange to have them disconnected or call forwarded to another extension. Rearrange whatever you must in order to feel comfortable in the room.

Secrets of Worthwhile Preparation

- Rehearse your speech while standing on your feet.
- Learn to and practice starting slowly.
- Have a hidden clock.
- Make use of "Reserved" signs.
- Warm up your voice daily.
- Have a written introduction.
- Prepare for your question period. File your used speeches for later reference.

Ninety-nine percent of speakers could use more self-confidence when they start their presentations! —Peter Urs Bender

There are two things people want more than sex and money–recognition and praise. —Mary Kay Ash

Remember–in presenting perception is reality. —Peter Urs Bender

Leadership is not about leading armies – it's about leading yourself.
SCHOBERLIN,
Zurich, Switzerland

This book is an informative and practical tool to establish your Main Vision.
MAXWELL,
London, England

National Best Seller

LEADERSHIP

FROM WITHIN

Check Results

Know Yourself

Leadership from Within™

Vision & Passion

Communicate

Take Risks

Peter Urs Bender

Your ideas are very clear. When reading your book it was like reading my own mind.
BJARNI INGIBERGSSON,
Rekjavik, Iceland

Attitudes + Behaviour = Results. Bender writes with clarity. No waste of words!
PICKWICK,
Toronto, Canada

Leadership From Within

Most people see leadership as the act of leading others. In keynotes, seminars and his book *Leadership From Within* Peter Urs Bender says that leadership "begins with leading ourselves." It starts with understanding our values and finding our vision and passion, then taking action and communicating effectively to create results. Every organisation needs staff that expresses this "leader-within". Those who move past their fears, take responsibility, make decisions, and create positive change. There is no limit to the growth we can achieve together when we develop the leader in each of us.

Analyse the five steps of becoming a more effective leader.

THE RELATIONSHIP BETWEEN EFFORT AND RETURN

Many of us start projects but do not complete them. We have great ideas but fail to reach our goals.

This is partly because we do not get results fast enough. We work hard for a time. But the effort we put in is greater than the results we get back, so we stop.

Success reinforces progress. It encourages us to keep going. Without it, our confidence begins to decline. We start to doubt ourselves, questioning the benefit of what we are doing. We think it will not work—and then we pull out before it does.

But look out! This is a trap! Why? Because of the principle of "Effort and Return." The following graph shows what I mean.

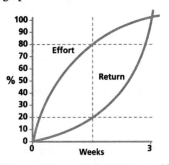

Bender believes that the key to success is knowing yourself. On the following page we offer a **free personality quiz**. For more help, visit Bender's website at:

www.PeterUrsBender.com

Peter Urs Bender's Guide to Strengths and Weaknesses of Personality Types

Each personality type has different strengths & weaknesses. Here are some things to watch for in yourself, and in the people you work with.

Type	Strengths	Potential Weaknesses
Analytical	Thinking	Excludes feelings from decisions
	Thorough	Goes too far; perfectionist
	Disciplined	Too rigid or demanding of self/others
Amiable	Supportive	Tends to conform to wishes of others
	Patient	No time boundaries; things do not get done
	Diplomatic	Not assertive or directive
Driver	Independent	Has trouble operating with others
	Decisive	Does not take time to consider other perspectives
	Determined	Domineering; too focused on doing it "my way"
Expressive	Good communicator	Talks too much
	Enthusiastic	Comes on too strong
	Imaginative	Dreamer; unrealistic

Peter Urs Bender's Guide to How Personality Theorists Have Described the Four Most Common Personality Types

(Correlations are approximate)

David W. Merrill and Roger H. Reid, *Personal Styles and Effective Performance*	Analytical	Amiable	Driver	Expressive
Hippocrates/Galen (Medieval Four Temperaments)	Melancholic	Phlegmatic	Choleric	Sanguine
Tim LaHaye/Littauer	Melancholic Perfect Phlegmatic	Peaceful Choleric	Powerful Sanguine	Popular
Carl G. Jung	Thinker	Feeler	Director	Intuitor
Myers-Briggs	Introvert/ Thinker	Introvert/ Feeler	Extrovert/ Thinker	Extrovert/ Feeler
Peter F. Drucker	Thought Man	People Man	Action Man	Front Man
The Stuart Atkins LIFO System	Conserving-Holding	Supporting-Giving	Controlling-Taking	Adapting-Dealing
DISC	Compliance	Steadiness	Dominance	Influencing
Robert E. Lefton	Submissive-Hostile	Submissive-Warm	Dominant-Hostile	Dominant-Warm
True Colors(TM)	Gold	Blue	Green	Orange
Bird Symbols	Owl	Dove	Eagle	Peacock
Animal Symbols	Beaver	Golden Retriever	Lion	Otter
Other well-known expressions	Processor Cognitive Logistical Compliance	Helper Interpersonal Supporter Submission	Boss Behavioral Commander Dominance	Impulsive Affective Socializer Inducement

...it's hard not to pick up lots of usable advice from this book.
The Globe and Mail

When it comes to marketing, originality counts.
Marketing Magazine

The book is easy to follow, contains many examples and quotes, and offers excellent advice.
Canada One Online Magazine

National Best Seller

SECRETS OF

P·O·W·E·R

MARKETING

Peter Urs Bender
& George Torok

SPM is an entertaining, idea-packed inspirational guide...
The Business Executive

The ideas they offer are simple and practical tools.
The Financial Post

The writers are old pros whose success validates their advice
Your Office

Zig when everyone else Zags.
The Star

Secrets of Power Marketing

Millions have been raised to believe "if you build a better mousetrap, the world will beat a path to your door." But this is a lie! To thrive in business, you must be seen and heard. People must talk about you, know where to find you and believe in the value of what you offer. In *Secrets of Power Marketing* Peter Urs Bender and George Torok explain how this exposure comes from marketing—in essence, belief in yourself and the ability communicate it to others. "Marketing is everything you do in life *that expresses who you are, what you do and creates a perception of your value.*" You cannot **not** market. The most successful companies and individuals are those who have learned the secrets of how to do it effectively.

Five areas where you can improve your marketability:

PERCEPTION

If you meet your client for the first time after you just walked through a drenching rainstorm he will forever think of you as the drowned rat.

RELATIONSHIPS

Strong relationships with your clients and prospects will earn you more business than price and quality alone.

MEDIA

A good reputation is built over a lifetime. But the power of the media can make you a hero or a zero in no time.

LEVERAGE

Spend $1 and you will get 80 cents in value. But if you want 100 times your return—be creative and tap into your intangible resources.

DATABASE MARKETING

Show me the names in your database and I know who you are.

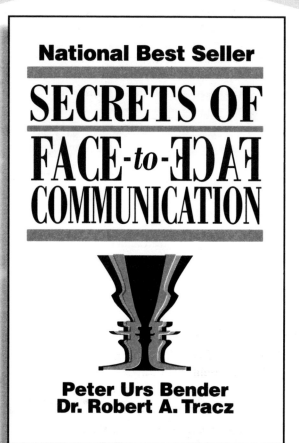

National Best Seller

SECRETS OF
FACE-*to*-FACE
COMMUNICATION

Peter Urs Bender
Dr. Robert A. Tracz